Black Adolescence

Current Issues and Annotated Bibliography

Black Adolescence

Current Issues and Annotated Bibliography

by
The Consortium for Research
on Black Adolescence
with
Velma McBride Murry
and assistance from
Georgie Winter

G.K. Hall & Co.
Boston, Massachusetts

First published 1990
by G.K. Hall & Co.
70 Lincoln Street
Boston, Massachusetts 02111

10 9 8 7 6 5 4 3

Library of Congress Cataloging-in-Publication Data

Black adolescence : current issues and annotated bibliography / by
The Consortium for Research on Black Adolescence with Velma McBride
Murry and assistance from Georgie Winter

      p. cm.
   Includes bibliographical references (p.)
   ISBN 0-8161-9080-1
   1. Afro-American teenagers – Bibliography.
   2. Adolescence – Bibliography.
 I. University of Connecticut. Consortium for Research on
Black Adolescence.
Z1361.N39B495 1990
[E185.86]
016.30523'5'08996073 – dc20   89-26995
                                          CIP

MANUFACTURED IN THE UNITED STATES OF AMERICA

Contents

v

Acknowledgments

The Consortium for Research on Black Adolescence (CROBA) wishes to acknowledge the financial support of the William T. Grant Foundation and especially the guidance of Linda M. Pickett, former vice president for program and assistant secretary to whom this work is dedicated. We also wish to acknowledge the support of the School of Family Studies and the Department of Sociology, the University of Connecticut; the assistance of Sherry O'Brien, Assistant Readers' Services Librarian, the Madeleine Clark Wallace Library, Wheaton College; the support of Lena Bailey, Dean, College of Home Economics of the Ohio State University, Columbus, Ohio; and the assistance of Lula Petty, coordinator, reading and study skills, African-American Institute, Northeastern University. A special thanks goes to Georgie Winter, research assistant to CROBA, whose critical judgment and care greatly enhanced this document.

Introduction

PATRICIA BELL-SCOTT
UNIVERSITY OF CONNECTICUT

Black Adolescence: Current Issues and Annotated Bibliographies is a revised
and expanded version of a document prepared by the Consortium for
Research on Black Adolescence (CROBA) in 1987. Though this document
was initially prepared for internal use by CROBA and a small circle of
colleagues, some 200 requests from social service professionals, academic
and public libraries, students, teachers, policy makers, and community
activists were received within nine months of the first limited printing. We
believe that these requests reflect a growing, general interest in Black
adolescents that has been fueled by several factors:

1. *A proportional increase in the Black adolescent population.* According to
   the 1980 U.S. Census, nearly 50 percent of the total Black population is
   under 23 years of age, with 10.5 million being under 19. Hence, the
   experiences and needs of Black adolescents are felt by both Black
   America and the wider society.

2. *The social and economic costs of the complex problems experienced by
   Black adolescents and their families.* Several recent works such as
   Jonathan Kozol's *Illiteracy* (1987), Douglas Glasgow's *The Black
   Underclass* (1980), and William J. Wilson's *The Truly Disadvantaged*
   (1987) document alarming rates and dire consequences of illiteracy,
   substance abuse, intergenerational unemployment, and teen
   parenthood.

3. *The desire of policy makers, helping professionals, and community
   activists to promote successful development among Black adolescents.*
   Recently established commissions and pilot projects by the Ford
   Foundation, The Carnegie Corporation of New York, the William T.
   Grant Foundation, the MacArthur Foundation, state governments,
   universities, community agencies, and civil rights organizations are

1

important indicators of the concern for and efforts to improve the well-being of minority and poor youth.

It is these factors, coupled with the demand for the original document, which suggested to CROBA the need for a reference book of this type.

In terms of format, *Black Adolescence* is divided into eleven sections, covering the topics of psychosocial development, psychological health, physical health, drug abuse, suicide, academic performance, education and occupational choice, employment, family-adolescent relationships, sexuality and contraception, and teen parenting. Each of the eleven sections is divided into three parts: (1) a summary, (2) annotated references, and (3) other references. The summary, which introduces each section, discusses trends and themes in the literature, critiques methodology where appropriate, and identifies gaps in the knowledge base. The annotated references, which typically contain a statement of purpose, description of the sample, and statement of findings, represent many of the most significant empirical and theoretical works published since 1975. The other reference section is composed of relevant sources which do not focus exclusively on Black adolescence.

In terms of working definitions, adolescence refers to those biological, cognitive, psychological, and social processes and experiences occurring between childhood and adulthood. Thus, research covering early, middle, and late adolescence (i.e., roughly ages 10 through 22) has been included. By the term Black, we refer to persons of African descent residing in the U.S. from any region, income level, family type, and cultural background.

Despite our efforts to examine the uniqueness and diversity among Black adolescents, several problems in the research base emerge from this work. These problems include: (1) the absence of a unifying theoretical framework to which empirical research is linked; (2) the use of conceptual models that ignore the intersection of race, class, gender, family context and culture, as well as the role of mediating variables in adolescent behavior; (3) the lack of attention to and controls for within-group differences; (4) the absence of research on middle-class and psychologically competent or well-adjusted adolescents and their families; and (5) a longstanding focus on individual deviancy and family pathology. Specific issues of concern include:

1. *The use of vague or poorly operationalized constructs such as "ghetto youth culture."* Such terms do not convey the extent to which race and class may be confounding variables. Ethnographic studies suggest that "ghetto youth culture" (as often reflected in gang membership and anti-social behavior) is not unique to Black adolescents, but is operable among urban and economically disadvantaged youth across all racial and ethnic lines (Gibbs, 1988; Myers, 1982).

2. *The assumption of homogeneity among Black adolescents and their families.* Few studies consider the "multiple ecologies" of Black adolescent development created by regional (e.g., rural southern versus urban northeastern), ethnocultural (e.g., Haitian, Creole-speaking versus Puerto-Rican, Spanish-speaking), or socioeconomic background (e.g., working-class versus middle-class), or by family type and personality differences. Common practice assumes a low-income, English-speaking heritage for all Black youth (Bell-Scott and Taylor, 1989; Myers, 1982).

3. *The use of unbalanced research designs and biased instruments.* Few studies match subjects along class, age, and family structural variables or consider the appropriateness of instruments developed on White middle-class subjects. The tendency is to compare Black adolescents from poor or single-parent families with White youths from working or middle-class, two-parent families by employing instruments of questionable or untested validity across race, class, or gender lines (McKenry et al., 1989).

4. *The use of nonrandom, nonrepresentative samples from which results are broadly generalized.* Seldom are samples drawn from a population that includes the range of family types, personalities and socio-cultural and behavioral variables present in most Black communities. There remains an overreliance on captive and clinical populations (e.g., adolescents and families involved in treatment programs). Representative samples, which are less conveniently obtained, are extremely rare (Gibbs, 1985).

There is clearly a need for: (1) theory development; (2) studies based on representative samples and carefully operationalized constructs; and (3) multi-method strategies that are sensitive to the complex interrelationships between and among the variables of race, culture, class, age, gender, and family structure. Studies that explore the issues of Black adolescent competency, coping behavior, decision-making, sibling relationships, extended family relationships, occupational development, and sexual socialization are sorely needed. It is hoped that *Black Adolescence* might be a useful tool in addressing these critical gaps in the knowledge base.

References

Bell-Scott, P., and Taylor, R.L. (1989). The multiple ecologies of Black adolescent development. (Special issue on Black adolescents.) *Journal of Adolescent Research, 4*(2), 119-124.

Gibbs, J.T. (1985). Black adolescents and youth: An endangered species. *American Journal of Orthopsychiatry, 54,* 6-21.

Gibbs, J.T. (1988). *Young, Black, and male in America: An endangered species.* Dover, Mass.: Auburn House.

McKenry, P. et al. (1989). Research on Black adolescents: A legacy of cultural bias. *Journal of Adolescent Research, 4*(2), 254-264.

Myers, H. (1982). Research on the Afro-American family: a critical review. In B.A. Bass, S.E. Wyatt, and G.J. Powell (Eds.), *The Afro-American family: Assessment, treatment, and research* (pp. 35-68). New York: Harcourt Brace Jovanovich.

Psychosocial Development

RONALD L. TAYLOR
UNIVERSITY OF CONNECTICUT

Summary

The role of significant others (i.e., as role models and reference groups) in the psychosocial development of children and youth has long been a topic of interest and research among students of human development. Research has shown that significant others are not only a source of attitudes, beliefs, and values among adolescents but are critical components of their self/identity formation. The concept of significant others has various parameters and has been used by many theorists to denote those individuals or groups who exert a major influence on the attitudes of individuals by: (1) communicating the norms, values, and expectations of the culture or society in which they live; (2) defining the behavior that is considered to be appropriate to the culture or society in which the individual resides; (3) modeling the appropriate attitudes and behavior; and (4) providing the necessary information about the environment to the individuals under their influence (Shade, 1983).

Despite consensus that significant others are important in the psychosocial development of children and youths, theory and research in this area remain at the formative stages. The literature is replete with confusion over conceptual differences between key terms and disagreements regarding appropriate methodology for empirical investigations. The manner in which role models and other significant individuals are selected and rendered useful by children and youth in their attempts to cultivate features of their personal and social identities has received scant attention in the literature, as have the specific qualities of significant others that make them significant in the eyes of children. Measures of known validity and reliability have yet to be developed and the bulk of the research on the topic has relied on survey instruments and occasionally formal interviews. As a consequence, much of the work available is limited in breadth and depth of insight. In sum, though a considerable literature now exists on the topic, no coherent picture of the significance of adults in adolescents' lives has emerged. Indeed, the preponderance of research available is limited to the study of White children and youths; only a handful of studies has sought to investigate the influence of significant others in the lives of Black children and youths.

Most of the available literature, as it relates to the significant others of Black children and youth, can be usefully categorized in terms of research and writing that: (1) present a theoretical and/or conceptual treatment of the topic; (2) examine the institutional or sociocultural contexts that condition selection or identification with significant others; and (3) report general or specific findings on the attitudes and preferences of Black youth that reflect their reference group orientations or association with significant others. These categories are not mutually exclusive, since a single work may include all three characteristics.

Those interested in the theoretical and conceptual issues associated with the topic will find several publications particularly useful. Cross (1985) reviews the bulk of the literature relevant to Black children and youth published between 1939 and 1977, and identifies the major conceptual and methodological weaknesses of this body of work, as does Hare (1977) in his overview of the literature. Hauser's (1971) research on Black/White identity formation examines some of the theoretical assumptions, methods, and data relating to role model identification and identity development among these youths, and Taylor's (1986) synthesis of the theoretical and empirical literature includes a framework for analysis of the role of significant others in the psychosocial development of Black adolescents. In addition, Galbo's (1984) survey of the literature, while not exclusively devoted to Black youth, includes a useful summary of empirical findings, organized around major theoretical issues.

The community, family, and other institutional contexts, including the media, which structure or influence adolescent choices of significant others are examined in several works. Shade (1983) presents a brief discussion of these external processes, while Scanzoni (1971), Curry (1976; 1978), and Badaines (1976) examine the processes involved in the selection of and identification with family members and community persons as role models. The broadest coverage of the literature in this area is provided by Ianni (1983), who supplements his review with results from field work conducted in a number of communities. The socialization effects of the media via role models presented to Black adolescents are examined in several articles in a collection edited by Berry and Mitchell-Kernan (1982); and the differential impact of place of residence on role model preferences of Black youth is investigated in the study by Oberle, Stowers, and Falk (1978).

The single best source of national data on the attitudes and beliefs of Black youth on a variety of topics is the survey of high school seniors by Bachman, Johnston, Lloyd, and O'Malley (1981). Although not specifically about the significant others or reference group orientations of Black youth, the responses of these youth to a wide range of topics offer important insights into their attitudes, values, and beliefs. The political beliefs and value orientations of Black youth, derived from experience and association with significant others, are examined in the research by Long (1983) and Taylor (1977), each of whom provides a useful research strategy for investigating these issues.

Annotated References

Bachman, J. G., Johnston, L.D., and O'Malley, P.M. (1981). *Monitoring the future: Questionnaire responses from the nation's high school seniors, 1980.* Ann Arbor: University of Michigan, Institute for Social Research.

This volume is the sixth in a series that presents descriptive results from a national survey of high school seniors enrolled in 107 public and 20 private high schools throughout the coterminous United States. The project was designed to monitor changes in important values, behaviors, and lifestyle orientations of contemporary youth. The survey covered a wide range of topics and included some 1,300 variables. While drug use and related attitudes received the most extensive coverage in the survey, other subjects included attitudes about government, social institutions, race relations, changing roles for women, educational aspirations, occupational aims, and marital and family plans. More than 16,000 seniors participated in the project, and Black seniors represented approximately 12 percent of the sample.

Badaines, J. (1976). Identification, imitation, and sex-role preference in father-present and father-absent Black and Chicano boys. *Journal of Psychology, 92,* 15-24.

This is a two-part study of identification and imitation in 52 Black and Chicano seven-year-old boys. Part one investigated the effect of race of model and subject on imitation of behavior; part two investigated the effects of paternal status (i.e., father-absent or father-present in the home) on choice of male or female model and masculine sex-role preference. Subjects were exposed to filmed models performing various tasks. While Black subjects expressed a significant preference for Black models, no significant preference for Black, White or Chicano models was expressed by Chicano subjects. The investigator concludes that by age seven, masculine preference is well established, and it is more evident among father-present subjects.

Berry, G.L., and Mitchell-Kernan, C. (Eds.). (1982). *Television and the socialization of the minority child.* New York: Academic Press.

A collection of articles written by experts from a variety of disciplines on the role of the media in shaping the attitudes, language, and psychosocial development of minority children and youth. The editors present a conceptual overview of television and its role in the socialization of minority children, and identify broad cognitive and affective developmental issues as areas of central concern. Various chapters examine the influence of television on mental health, identity formation, and self-concept development among minority children. Also included are articles on research methodologies and appropriate strategies for illuminating the impact of television on minority group children.

Cross, W.E. (1985). Black identity: Rediscovering the distinction between personal identity and reference group orientations. In M.B. Spencer, G.K. Brookins, and W.R. Allen (Eds.), *Beginnings: The social and affective development of Black children* (pp. 155-171). Hillsdale, N.J.: Lawrence Erlbaum.

This is a critical review of the vast literature on personal identity and reference group orientations of Black children and youth from the period 1939-1977. In reviewing the work of this period, Cross contends that researchers have often failed to distinguish between Black self-concept (i.e., personal identity) and group identity or reference group orientation, with important consequences for research and theory in this area. It is argued that each construct requires a different phenomena. Failure to operationalize the two constructs in a manner that makes them readily discernible has resulted in erroneous interpretations of Black identity.

Curry, E.W. (1976). *Significant other influence and career decisions.* Volume 1, *Black and White male urban youth.* (Research and Development Series No. 107.) Columbus: Ohio State University, National Center for Research in Vocational Education. (ERIC Document Reproduction Service No. ED 159 332.)

An empirical investigation of the process by which parents and other individuals influence the educational and occupational plans of male high school sophomores. Data were collected from a sample of 247 subjects, their parents, and individuals identified by the subjects as having been influential in affecting their educational and occupational career plans. Among the major findings were that: (1) both Black and White youth identified similar numbers of significant others for their career decisions, and such persons listed tended to be of the same race as the respondents; (2) the familial network provided the majority of significant others for both groups; and (3) extended family members were generally of greater importance for Black than White youth.

Curry, E.W. (1978). *Significant other influence and career decisions.* Volume 2, *Black and White female urban youth.* (Research and Development Series

No. 138.) Columbus: Ohio State University, National Center for Research in Vocational Education. (ERIC Document Reproduction Service No. ED 159 333.)

A companion study to an earlier work on Black and White male urban youth which investigates the formation of career plans among Black and White female youth, using the theoretical and empirical framework derived from a modified version of the Wisconsin Model of status attainment. Data were collected from a sample of racially balanced, female high school sophomores, and from their significant others, on the latter's occupational and educational expectations for the subjects. Among the major findings were: Significant other variables were the most accurate predictors of career-choice variables; The home-career expectation of females did not manifest strong effects on educational or occupational expectations; and Significant other variables did not affect educational and occupational expectations for females more strongly than for males. The implications of these findings for research and theory are presented.

Galbo, J.J. (1984). Adolescents' perceptions of significant adults: A review of the literature. *Adolescence, 19,* 951-970.

A review of research on adolescent perceptions of the influence of significant others in self development. The review is presented according to the following topics: (1) Who are the significant adults with whom adolescents voluntarily associate? (2) What characteristics of significant others are identified by adolescents? (3) At what point do adolescents notice that particular adults are significant? (4) In what settings do adolescents associate with significant adults? (5) To what extent are teachers perceived as being significant adults? (6) What relationship exists between adolescents' perceptions of adults and alienation? The author discusses the major limitations of research on these topics and underscores the need for more sophisticated research designs and analyses.

Hare, B.R. (1977). Black and White child self-esteem in social science: An overview. *Journal of Negro Education, 46,* 141-156.

Hare presents an overview of the literature on Black self-esteem and identifies the problems associated with assessing the role of significant others in the process. Hare contends that most studies of self-evaluation involving children are limited in their applicability to subjects across class and racial lines; fail to specify where and when different individual and group influences interact or act distinctively in affecting the child's self-evaluation, and how significant others differentially contribute to the self-evaluation of the subject. Two theoretical models for child self-concept studies are presented to address these problems and to stimulate new research in this area.

Hauser, S.T. (1971). *Black and White identity formation: Studies in the psychosocial development of lower socioeconomic class adolescent boys.* New York: John Wiley.

This monograph presents multiple facets of method, data, and theoretical models in reporting the results of a longitudinal study of Black and White identity formation. A total of 23 Black and White male youths, ranging in age from 14-16 were interviewed and tested in the study. Hauser found Black adolescents to have different identity formation patterns from White adolescents, and devotes a large part of the study to identifying the sources or causes of these differential patterns. The work contains some insightful observations on the significance of role models in identity formation and useful recommendations for future research on the topic.

Ianni, F.A.J. (1983). *Home, school and community in adolescent education.* New York: Columbia University, Institute for Urban and Minority Education. (ERIC Document Reproduction Service No. ED 336 300.)

This is a study of the transition from childhood to adulthood in a variety of social contexts, using methods drawn from field ethnography, clinical psychoanalysis, and survey research. The study explores the connections and conflicts between and among the institutional contexts – work and schooling, the family and the peer group, the criminal justice system and other social contexts – as these contribute to the quality of psychosocial development among youth. This volume contains an excellent review of the massive literature on the topic and presents a useful model for analysis of critical influences and conditions which shape the psychosocial economy of Black inner-city youths.

Long, S. (1983). Psychopolitical orientations of White and Black youth: A test of five models. *Journal of Black Studies, 13,* 439-457.

This is a review of the literature and an empirical investigation of five models of psychopolitical orientations among a large sample of Black and White youths enrolled in five inner-city schools located in a large mid-western city. Major differences in psychopolitical orientations between White and Black adolescents involved in the study were observed. Such differences were explained on the basis of differential levels of perceived self-competence or esteem, and differential perceptions of political reality on the part of Black and White youth. Competing explanations of racial differences in political orientations received weak to moderate support in this study.

Oberle, W.H., Stowers, K.R., and Falk, W.W. (1978). Place of residence and the role model preferences of Black boys and girls. *Adolescence, 13,* 13-20.

This is a brief review of the literature and an investigation of the effect of place of residence on role model preference of Black youth. A total of 434 Black sophomores from urban and rural communities were participants in the study. The study found that place of residence was significantly related to the role model preferences of respondents. Specifically, it was found that urban boys preferred different role models from rural boys, and that urban girls preferred different models from rural girls. The investigators conclude that place of residence cannot be regarded as a variable which is unimportant to the process in which educational and occupational goals of youth become crystallized.

Scanzoni, J.H. (1971). *The Black family in modern society.* Boston: Allyn & Bacon.

Although the substantive focus of this volume is on structure and dynamics of Black families, it contains several important chapters on the influence of parents as role models and significant others for Black adolescents. Based on a survey of 400 Black households in a large midwestern city, and employing a quasigenerational model, this study describes and analyzes relationships experienced by the respondents with their parents and with other adults while they were still adolescents, and assesses the influence of these relationships on current attitudes and behavior in their role as parents. The extent to which the respondents' own children identified with them as role models was also investigated. Scanzoni discusses the significance of these findings for theory and practice.

Shade, B.J. (1983). The social success of Black youth: the impact of significant others. *Journal of Black Studies, 14,* 137-150.

This is a general discussion and review of the literature on the differential role of parents, peers, and the media in shaping the attitudes and behavior of Black youth. Shade notes the instrumental role of Black mothers in fostering a sense of competence and achievement in Black children, and the more expressive function of Black fathers aimed at introducing the child to sex roles, values and methods of adaptation in the wider society. Television's role in reinforcing stereotypic images of Afro-Americans, and its presentation of negative role models are also discussed, as are the negative influences of peer groups and street culture on Black adolescents.

Taylor, R.L. (1977). The orientational others and value preferences of Black college youth. *Social Science Quarterly, 57,* 797-810.

This article reports results from an investigation of the significant others and value preferences of Black students enrolled in a large New England university. The investigator distinguishes between "orientational others" (i.e., others with whom the respondent had a history of relationships) and role-specific significant others (i.e., others with whom the individual's relationship and interaction tends to be situationally determined). The study found that, when their role as student was considered, faculty and administrators defined the modal hierarchy of significant others for Black college students; however, when their behavior and attitudes were considered within a more general non-specific, transituational context, the order of preference was observed to change, such that family and friends emerged to occupy major positions of importance. In both normative content and choice of significant others, the modal value orientation of these Black college youth gave high priority to traditional achievement values.

Taylor, R.L. (1986). Black youth and psychosocial development: A conceptual framework. In R. Staples (Ed.), *The Black family: Essays and studies* (3d edition) (pp. 201-210). Belmont, Calif: Wadsworth (Reprinted from *Journal of Black Studies*, 1976, *6*, 353-372.

This is a review of the general theoretical literature and research on role modeling behavior. A conceptual framework for analysis of modeling behavior among Black youth is presented. Two types of role models are conceptually distinguished: exemplary and symbolic models. The former refers to specific persons who serve as examples by means of which specific skills and behavior patterns are acquired, while the latter refers to a set of attributes or ideal qualities that may or may not be linked directly with any one particular person as such. In addition, the relationship between a given youth and his or her model is conceptualized in terms of type, content, and scope of their relationship. With the use of this conceptual framework, Taylor reports findings from in-depth interviews with a sample of Black male youth.

Other References

Bandura, A. (1978). Self-system in reciprocal determinism. *American Psychologist, 33*, 344-358.

Biddle, B.J., Bank, B.J., Anderson, D.S., Haughe, R., Keats, D.M., Keats, J.A., Marlin, M.M., and Valantin, S. (1985). Social influence, self-referent identity labels, and behavior. *Sociological Quarterly, 26*, 159-185.

Bridgeman, B., and Burbach, H. (1976). Effects of Black and White peer models on academic expectations and actual performance of fifth-grade students. *Journal of Experimental Education, 45,* 9-12.

Carpenter, P.G., and Western, J.S. (1982). Aspirations for higher education. *Australian Journal of Education, 26,* 266-278.

Carpenter, P.G., and Western, J.S. (1983). The facilitation of attainment aspirations. *Australian and New Zealand Journal of Sociology, 19,* 305-318.

Carver, C., Ganellen, R.J., Froming, W.J., and Chambers, W. (1983). Modeling: An analysis in terms of category accessibility. *Journal of Experimental Social Psychology, 19,* 403-421.

Castine, S.C., and Roberts, G.C. (1974). Modeling in the socialization of the Black athlete. *International Review of Sport Sociology, 9,* 59-74.

Coates, D.L. (1985). Relationships between self-concept measures and social network characteristics for Black adolescents. *Journal of Early Adolescence, 5,* 319-338.

Coates, D.L. (1987). Gender differences in the structure and support characteristics of Black adolescents' social networks. *Sex Roles, 17,* 667-687.

Curtis, R.L. (1974). Parents and peers: Serendipity in a study of shifting reference sources. *Social Forces, 52,* 368-375.

Evans, R.C. (1987). Adolescent sexual activity, pregnancy, and child rearing: Attitudes of significant others on risk factors. (Special Issue). *Child and Youth Services, 9,* 75-93.

Erkut, S., and Mokros, J.R. (1984). Professors as models and mentors for college students. *American Educational Research Journal, 21,* 399-417.

Fehrenbach, P.A., Miller, D.J., and Thelen, M.H. (1979). Importance of consistency of modeling behavior upon imitation: A comparison of single and multiple models. *Journal of Personality and Social Psychology, 37,* 1412-1417.

Gaston, J.C. (1986). The destruction of the young male: The impact of popular culture and organized sports. *Journal of Black Studies, 16,* 369-384.

Garbarino, J., Burston, N., Raber, S., Russell, R., and Crouter, A. (1978). The social maps of children approaching adolescence: Studying the ecology of youth development. *Journal of Youth and Adolescence, 7,* 417-428.

Gottfredson, G.D. (1982). *Role models, bonding, and delinquency: An examination of competing perspectives*. (Report No. 337.) Baltimore, Md.: Johns Hopkins University, Center for Social Organization of Schools.

Gottfried, A.E., and Katz, P.A. (1977). Influence of belief, race and sex similarities between child observers and models on attitudes and observational learning. *Child Development, 48,* 1395-1400.

Greene, J.R., and Bynum, T. (1982). T.V. crooks: Implications of latent role models for theories of delinquency. *Journal of Criminal Justice, 10,* 177-190.

Gresham, F.M., and Nage, R.J. (1980). Social skills training with children: Responsiveness to modeling and coaching as a function of peer orientation. *Journal of Counseling and Clinical Psychology, 48,* 718-729.

Haller, A.O., and Woelfel, J. (1972). Significant others and their expectations: Concepts and instruments to measure interpersonal influences on status aspirations. *Rural Sociology, 37,* 591-622.

Hosford, R.E. (1980). Self as-a-model: A cognitive social learning technique. *The Counseling Psychologist, 9,* 45-61.

Howie, A.M. (1975). Effects of belief exposure to symbolic model behavior on the information-processing strategies of internally and externally oriented children. *Developmental Psychology, 11,* 325-333.

Hunt, L.L., and Hunt, J.G. (1975). Race and the father-son connection: the conditional relevance of father absence for the orientations and identities of adolescent boys. *Social Problems, 23*(1), 35-52.

Hunt, L.L., and Hunt, J.G. (1977). Race, father identification and achievement orientation: the subjective side of the father-son connection, a research note. *Youth and Society, 9*(1), 113-120.

Johnson, W.E. (1976). Imitative aggression as a function of role of model, race of target and socioeconomic status of observer. *Dissertation Abstracts International, 37,* 3150-3151B.

Levinson, R., Powell, B., and Stellman, L.C. (1986). Social location, significant others, and body image among adolescents. *Social Psychology Quarterly, 49,* 330-337.

Levy, S.G. (1974). Racial differences in political orientations: Identification vs. alienation. *Personality and Social Psychology Bulletin, 1,* 333-341.

Macke, A.S., and Morgan, W.R. (1978). Maternal employment, race, and work orientation of high school girls. *Social Forces, 57,* 187-204.

14

Masters, J.C., Martin, F., Arend, R., Grotevant, H., and Clark, L. (1979). Modeling and labeling as integrated determinants of children's sex-typed imitative behavior. *Child Development, 50,* 364-371.

Mettlin, C. (1975). Detecting agents of interpersonal influence. *Interchange, 6,* 38-46.

Miller, L., and Roll, S. (1977). Adolescent males' ratings of being understood by fathers, best friends, and significant others. *Psychological Reports, 40,* 1079-1082.

Miller, T.W. (1983). Identification process and sensory impact of children's television programming on the preschool child. *Child Study Journal, 13,* 203-207.

Nolle, D.B. (1972). Changes in Black sons and daughters: A panel analysis of Black adolescents' orientations toward their fathers. *Journal of Marriage and the Family, 34*(3), 443-447.

Oberle, W.H. (1974). Role models of Black and White rural youth at two stages of adolescence. *Journal of Negro Education, 43,* 234-244.

Parton, D.A., and Siebold, J.R. (1975). Nurturance and imitation: The mediating role of attraction. *Developmental Psychology, 11,* 859-860.

Perry, D.G., and Perry, L.C. (1975). Observational learning in children: Effects of sex of model and subject's sex role behavior. *Journal of Personality and Social Psychology, 31,* 1083-1088.

Porter-Gehrie, C. (1979). Models of adulthood: An ethnographic study of an adolescent peer group. *Journal of Youth and Adolescence, 8,* 253-267.

Raskin, P.A., and Israel, A.C. (1981). Sex role imitation in children: Effects of sex of child, sex of model and sex role appropriateness of modeled behavior. *Sex Roles, 7,* 1067-1077.

Rochberg-Halton, E. (1984). Object relations, role models and cultivation of the self. *Environment and Behavior, 16,* 335-368.

Rosenberg, M. (1976). Which significant others? In J. Heiss (Ed.), *Family roles and interaction: An anthology* (pp. 363-393). Chicago: Rand McNally.

Rothbaum, F., Zigler, E., and Hyson, M.C. (1981). Modeling, praising and collaborating: Effects of adult behavior on children of the same sex and opposite sex. *Journal of Experimental Child Psychology, 31,* 403-423.

Schwartz, S.H., and Ames, R.E. (1977). Positive and negative referent others as sources of influence: A case of helping. *Sociometry, 40,* 12-21.

Scritchfield, S.A., and Picou, J.S. (1982). The structure of significant others influence on status aspirations: Black-White variations. *Sociology of Education, 55,* 22-30.

Sims, S.A. (1978). Effects of modeling processes and resources on sharing among Black children. *Psychological Reports, 43,* 463-473.

Smith, E.J. (1976). Reference group perspective and the vocational maturity of lower socioeconomic Black youth. *Journal of Vocational Behavior, 8,* 321-336.

Torrance, E.P. (1983). Role of mentors in creative achievement. *Creative Child and Adult Quarterly, 8,* 8-15.

Turner, S.M., and Forehand, R. (1976). Imitative behavior as a function of success-failure and racial-socioeconomic factors. *Journal of Applied Social Psychology, 6,* 40-47.

Weiland, A., and Stephen, W. (1978). The effects of race on imitation. *Journal of Genetic Psychology, 133,* 277-285.

Weston, R. (1977). Level of Black awareness, race of experimenter, race of model and modeling task in vicarious learning. *Dissertation Abstracts International, 38,* 23908.

Willie, C.V. (1984). The role of mothers in the lives of outstanding scholars: A guest editorial. *Journal of Family Issues, 5,* 291-306.

Wilson, J.P., and Petruska, R. (1984). Motivation, model attributes and prosocial behavior. *Journal of Personality and Social Psychology, 46,* 458-468.

Zimmerman, B.J., and Ringle, J. (1981). Effects of model persistence and statements of confidence on children's self-efficacy and problem solving. *Journal of Education Psychology, 73,* 485-493.

Psychological Health

HOWARD P. RAMSEUR
MASSACHUSETTS INSTITUTE OF TECHNOLOGY

".. . the Negro has no possible basis for a healthy self-esteem and every incentive for self-hatred."

> A. Kardiner and L. Ovesey, *The Mark of Oppression* (1951), p. 297.

".. . the experience of being black in a society dominated by whites does *not,* as is sometimes incorrectly assumed, lead to deep and corrosive personal demoralization. Blacks live with greater stress, but they have the personal and social resources to maintain a perspective which keeps the stress external, and not permit it to become internalized or to disrupt personal integration."

> J. Veroff, E. Douvan, and R.A. Kulka, *The Inner American* (1981), p. 437.

Summary

The traditional view in psychology, sociology, social work, and psychiatry of Black adolescent mental health is well summarized by the quote from Kardiner and Ovesey (1951) above; that is, given the social and cultural conditions under which Black Americans live, psychological health is an impossibility. Therefore, it has seemed irrelevant for traditional social scientists to examine the characteristics of psychological health for Blacks, adolescent or adult. And, in fact, the focus of traditional social science theory and research about Black youth has been on low self-esteem, self-hatred, and social pathology.

What are the psychological and social characteristics of psychologically healthy Black American adolescents? How do these characteristics change throughout adolescence? These are important questions, but ones that until recently have never been comprehensively addressed. Perhaps they have not been addressed because the idea that Black American adolescents or adults could be psychologically healthy is one that traditional social scientists and much of the lay public would find unacceptable.

The traditional theoretical model of personality and identity among Black youth and adults heavily focuses on self-conception; particularly the areas of self-esteem and racial (group) identity. While it has a number of variants, the basic model states that Blacks live in a racist White society, where they are viewed and treated as inferior, often living in poverty in a powerless community. It is argued that Black children internalize the beliefs and negative feelings about themselves and other Blacks held by the White community. Explanations of exactly how the internalization occurs and its precise impact on personality, self-esteem and identity and seem to vary with the theoretical orientation of the investigator. However, they almost universally find low self-esteem, negative racial identity, and in a number of studies repressed or explosive aggression. A number of empirical studies, including the classic Clark doll studies (1947), seem to support predictions of low self-esteem and self-hatred among Black children and youth (see Taylor, 1976b, for a review).

The 1960s and 1970s saw challenges to traditional theories about Black youth; particularly to notions that they had negative racial identities or global self-esteem lower than their White peers. The empirical supports of the traditional model were undermined by studies with findings that contradicted predictions about Black self-esteem and racial identity. (See Taylor, 1976a; Porter and Washington, 1979 for reviews.) For example, Black children and adolescents have been shown to have levels of self-esteem and psychosocial adjustment equal to their White peers (Allen, 1985; Gibbs, 1985; Looney and Lewis, 1983). In addition, Cross (1985) also points out that Black youth have been shown to have positive racial (group) identities in a majority of studies done since 1939. Porter and Washington (1979) argue that studies done since the 1960s find Black adolescents and adults showing a clear shift to a more positive racial self-esteem (identity). Veroff, Douvan, and Kulka (1981) show similar findings on self-esteem for Black adults.

One recent trend in this literature has been the attempt to understand the bases of positive self-esteem and self-concept among Black youth. Barnes (1980) suggests that under certain conditions the Black family and community act as a mediator or filter of negative images and messages for the Black child. Taylor (1976b) and Gibbs (1985) emphasize the immediate Black social context of Black children and adolescents as their primary source of social comparisons and self-evaluation, and therefore often positive self-concept. Porter and Washington (1979) survey a number of models relevant to understanding positive self-esteem and racial identity among Black adolescents.

Although some social scientists have moved beyond the traditional view and pointed to sources and mechanisms underlying positive Black self-esteem, which is certainly one aspect of psychological health, they have not constructed a more general model of healthy psychological adjustment or development among Black adolescents. This is perhaps a reflection of the lack of consensus and conceptual clarity in the field about what represents "psychological health" or "healthy development" for adolescents, Black or White. As Ramseur (in press) points out for Black adults and Blotcky and Looney (1980) as well as Powers, Hauser, and Kilner (1989) indicate for Black and White adolescents, competing theories and empirical results leave us without a well-supported general model of health for either group.

Perhaps in reaction to the lack of a general model of Black adolescent psychological health, investigators have tended to focus on one of two areas: (1) specific aspects of psychological functioning defined as healthy (e.g., competence, positive self-esteem, or high-level coping); or (2) a single aspect of healthy development. Taylor's (1976a) discussion of a conceptual framework for understanding healthy identity development among Black adolescents is a case in point. An example of the first area would be a small group of studies that look at "competent," or "psychosocially successful" Black adolescents (Griffin and Korchin, 1980; Looney and Lewis, 1983; Lee, 1985). These studies examined high school or college-age Blacks who were found to have highly positive attitudes towards the self and feelings of efficacy, to exhibit good interpersonal relationships and skills, and to have good to high levels of academic achievement. They possessed many of the characteristics of the competent self discussed by Smith (1968) and others. Another aspect of healthy functioning, adapting to stress and "successful" coping styles among older Black adolescents are examined by Abatso (1985). In addition, Myers and King (1980) discuss stress and Black adolescent coping styles more generally and outline issues worthy of future investigation.

While researchers looking at competent Black adolescents have pointed to the significance of personal, social, and family correlates of competence, research in this area is plagued by many of the same problems which plague studies of self-esteem and other aspects of psychological health as well. Little theoretical discussion or conceptual clarity exists in the literature as to what personal competence is for Black adolescents. Empirical studies are generally not clearly linked to theory, have very small samples, use unvalidated methods, and tend to draw general conclusions from small evidence. In addition, interesting sex differences are often noted, but rarely pursued. More generally, the area of Black adolescent psychological health lacks a theoretical framework from which to create a general model of healthy functioning and development. Empirical studies that look at specific areas of healthy functioning over the different phases of adolescence for both male and female Black adolescents are also sorely needed.

Annotated References

Abatso, Y. (1985). The coping personality: A study of Black community college students. In M.B. Spencer, G.K. Brookins, and W.R. Allen (Eds.), *Beginnings: The social and affective development of Black children* (pp. 131-153). Hillsdale, N.J.: Lawrence Erlbaum.

This is an investigation of the personality characteristics, behavioral strategies, and academic achievement of "high coping" Black community college students. These students are contrasted to their Black peers defined as average or low copers. Coping is defined and measured as behavior associated with student attempts to master the academic demands of the classroom. Personality variables measured were self-concept of (academic) ability, locus of control, achievement motivation, and perception of the occupational/educational opportunity structure (as open or closed to advancement). Achievement was defined as year-end grade point average. Study sample was 120 Chicago community college students who filled out paper and pencil instruments in two sessions; data analysis was correlational. High copers had higher self-concepts of ability and internal control sense and reported using a greater number and more diverse coping strategies than average or low copers. Coping, as defined here, was positively correlated to achievement.

Allen, W.R. (1985). Race, income and family dynamics: A study of adolescent male socialization processes and outcomes. In M.B. Spencer, G.K. Brookins, and W.R. Allen (Eds.), *Beginnings: The social and affective development of Black children* (pp. 273-292). Hillsdale, N.J.: Lawrence Erlbaum.

Allen examines, from a cross-cultural perspective, the family characteristics, interpersonal dynamics, and socialization outcomes for Black and White adolescent males (14-18 years of age) who were members of two-parent middle-income families. Based on individual interviews in 1974 with each family member in 120 Chicago families, the study found that both Black and White sons were "healthy" and "well-adjusted." It also found that Black families significantly differed from White ones in parents' child-rearing goals, practices, interpersonal relations, and views on socialization outcomes. A socialization complex model is proposed to explain adolescent socialization outcomes.

Barnes, E.J. (1980). The Black community as the source of positive self-concept for Black children: A theoretical perspective. In R. Jones (Ed.), *Black psychology* (pp. 106-130). New York: Harper & Row.

This literature review and theoretical discussion focuses on the issue of how a Black child develops a positive self-concept while growing up in American society. Barnes emphasizes the role of the Black community and family as mediators or processors of information and messages impinging on the Black child from the larger White community. The investigator argues that under certain conditions the Black community and families can "filter" out racist, destructive messages from White society and help Black children to develop positive self-esteem. Barnes provides preliminary data from a study using questionnaires and the Ethnic Pictures Test to examine the relationship between group identification and self-concept for Black children and their families.

Cross, W.E. (1985). Black identity: Rediscovering the distinction between personal identity and reference group orientation. In M.B. Spencer, G.K. Brookins, and W.R. Allen (Eds.), *Beginnings: The social and affective development of Black children* (pp. 151-174). Hillsdale, N.J.: Lawrence Erlbaum.

This is a review of 161 empirical studies of Black identity in children and adults that were published between 1939 and 1977. Cross asserts that personal identity and group identity (reference group orientation) are key concepts that have guided almost all studies. He surveys studies which examine the notion of negative Black identity (1939 to 1960s), and reputed changes in Black identity from 1968 to the present. Studies are classified as to whether they examine group identity, personal identity (and self-esteem), or measure both in the same sample. Reliability of methods and results are discussed. The author concludes that Black youth (and adults) have consistently had positive self-esteem, have a multi-faceted reference group orientation that is usually not negative, and that group identity and personal identity (especially self-esteem) have not been shown to be closely linked.

Gibbs, J.T. (1985). City girls: Psychosocial adjustment of urban Black adolescent females. *SAGE: A Scholarly Journal on Black Women, 2,* 28-36.

This is a brief review of the literature on the self-esteem and educational-vocational aspirations of Black adolescent females and a report of preliminary results of a study comparing Black and White adolescent females on measures of self-esteem, educational-vocational expectation, and on a global measure of adolescent psychological functioning. The nonrandom sample included 387 females in public schools in the San Francisco area, in grades 7-9, who filled out self-report inventories at school. Black girls were found to be as well-adjusted as White peers on a standardized scale of adolescent adjustment, to have equally positive self-esteem, and to have high educational aspirations and expectations.

Griffin, Q.D., and Korchin, S.J. (1980). Personality competence in Black male adolescents. *Journal of Youth and Adolescence, 9*(3), 211-227.

This is an empirical study of the nature and antecedents of personality competence in a sample of 23 Black male junior college students (18-21 years of age). Selected by Black and White professors as competent (13) or average (10), these subjects rated themselves on several self-image and personality description inventories. While both groups' ratings put them in the well-adjusted effectively functioning range on personality inventories, those males selected as competent were more ambitious, strove more vigorously for success, and were more inner- than outer-directed.

Lee, C.C. (1985). Successful rural Black adolescents: A psychosocial profile. *Adolescence, 20*(77), 129-142.

Lee investigates 68 rural, southern Black adolescents (8th-12th grade) nominated by their public-school teachers as academically and socially successful. Individual interviews explored their current psychological and social functioning as well as personal, family, and social factors that seemed to support them. These adolescents had positive, but realistic views of self, internal locus of control, supportive family networks, and positive but limited Black identities.

Looney, J.G., and Lewis, J.M. (1983). Competent adolescents from different socioeconomic and ethnic contexts. *Adolescent Psychiatry, 2,* 64-74.

This study compares two small samples of adolescents – one Black and working class ($n=11$) and another White and upper-middle class ($n=11$) – in eleven areas of psychological and social functioning. The White adolescents were studied prior to Blacks, and both groups had individual interviews. Their families were part of a larger study of competent families and subjects were selected from adolescents in those families. Black and White adolescents were found to have remarkably similar levels of adaptive functioning and attitudes, in all areas, ranging from self-esteem to social relationships, attitudes towards family, to academic achievement. See also Lewis and Looney, (1983) in Other References list for a discussion of the families of these adolescents.

Porter, J.R., and Washington, R.E. Black identity and self-esteem: A review of studies of black self-concept, 1968-1978. *Annual Review of Sociology, 1979,5,* 53-74.

A comprehensive review of empirical studies and theories about Black identity and self-esteem focused on 1968-1978. The authors divide self-esteem into two components: racial – Black or group identity; and personal, that is, global self-esteem. They survey the empirical studies of Black preschoolers, elementary students, adolescents and adults for both components. Examining racial self-esteem they argue that it is different now for Black adolescents (and adults) than in earlier years, with a shift to a more positive racial self-esteem. They review three theoretical approaches to understanding racial self-esteem: relative deprivation theory, the effects of subculture, and alienation. They also find that the bulk of studies of personal self-esteem show Black adolescents with equal or greater self-esteem when compared with their White peers. They survey four theoretical approaches to understanding personal self-esteem: social evaluation theory, locus of control, supportive Black subculture, and the "tangle of pathology" approach. They also point out that while a general reciprocal relationship between racial and personal self-esteem is often assumed, it is unproven, and in fact, contradicted by some studies.

Taylor, R.L. (1976a). Black youth and psychosocial development: A conceptual framework. *Journal of Black Studies, 6*(4), 353-372.

Taylor discusses the development of psychosocial identity among Black youth by focusing on the importance of role models in their active attempts to construct aspects of their social and personal identities. Relevant theory about identity development and role models during adolescence points to the importance of distinction between exemplary and symbolic role models. Case histories from 30 Black male college students are analyzed and point to father's changing importance as a role model.

Taylor, R.L. (1976b). Psychosocial development among Black children and youth: A reexamination. *American Journal of Orthopsychiatry, 46*(1), 4-19.

Taylor reviews traditional thinking and research about the development of Black self-identity, with emphasis on self-esteem of Black youth. The investigator points to recent studies that contradict traditional models and to major deficiencies in assumptions and methods of traditional studies. Alternative formulations for understanding the bases of positive self-esteem among Black youth, and the importance of social context in the development of self-identity are explored.

Other References

Baker, F.M. (1987, June) The Afro-American life cycle: Success, failure and mental health. *Journal of National Medical Association, 79*(6), 625-633.

Blotcky, M.J., and Looney, J.G. (1980). Normal female and male adolescent psychological development: An overview of theory and research. *Adolescent Psychiatry, 8*, 184-199.

Bowman, P.J., and Howard, C. (1985). Race-related socialization, motivation, and academic achievement: A study of Black youths in three-generation families. *Journal of the American Academy of Child Psychiatry, 24*(2), 134-141.

Calhoun, P.D. (1981). *Family factors in Black adolescent mental health.* Unpublished doctoral dissertation, George Peabody College for Teachers of Vanderbilt University, Nashville.

Clark, K.B., and Clark, M.K. (1947). Racial identification and preference in Negro children. In T. Newcomb and E. Hartley (Eds.), *Readings in Social Psychology* (pp. 602-611). New York: Henry Holt.

Comer, J.P. (1985). Black children and child psychiatry (Special Issue). *Journal of the American Academy of Child Psychiatry, 24*(2).

Edwards, O.L. (1976). Components of academic success: A profile of achieving Black adolescents. *Journal of Negro Education, 45,* 351-363.

Freeman, E.W., Rickels, K., Mudd, E., Huggins, G.R., and Garcia, C.R. (1982). Self-reports of emotional distress in a sample of urban Black high school students. *Psychological Medicine, 12,* 809-817.

Gary, L.E. (Ed.). (1978). *Mental health: A challenge to the Black community.* Philadelphia: Dorrance & Co., 6-21.

Gibbs, J.T. (1984). Black adolescents and youth: An endangered species. *American Journal of Orthopsychiatry, 54*(1), 6-21.

Group for Advancement of Psychiatry (1968). *Normal adolescence.* New York: Charles Scribner's.

Jones, E.E., and Korchin, S.J. (1982). *Minority mental health.* New York: Praeger.

Kardiner, A., and Ovesey, L. (1951). *The mark of oppression: Explorations in the personality of the American Negro.* New York: World Books.

Lewis, J.M., and Looney, J.G. (1983). *The long struggle: Well functioning working-class Black families.* New York: Brunner/Mazel.

Myers, H.F., and King, L.M. (1980). Youth of the Black underclass: Stress and mental health–Notes for an alternative formulation. *Fanon Center Journal, 1,* 1-27.

Ramseur, H. (in press). Psychologically healthy Black adults: A review of theory and research. In R. Jones (Ed.), *Black adult development and aging.* Berkeley, Calif.: Cobb and Henry.

Smith, E.J. (1982). The Black female adolescent: A review of the educational, career, and psychological literature. *Psychology of Women Quarterly, 6*(3), 261-288.

Smith, M.B. (1968). Competence and socialization. In J. Clausen (Ed.), *Socialization and society* (pp. 270-320). Boston: Little, Brown and Co.

Spencer, M.B. (1986). Minority children and mental health: Old perspectives and new proposals. In M.R. Isaacs (Ed.), *Developing mental health programs for minority youth and their families* (pp. 49-68). Washington, D.C.: Georgetown University Child Development Center, CASSP Technical Assistance Center.

Veroff, J., Douvan, E., and Kulka, R.A. (1981). *The inner American: A self-portrait from 1957 to 1976.* New York: Basic Books.

Physical Health

VELMA MCBRIDE MURRY
UNIVERSITY OF CONNECTICUT

Summary

Evaluation of existing data suggests that the health status of Black Americans, in general, and Black adolescents specifically, has not improved over time. In a comprehensive, longitudinal investigation of health stability and change Brunswick (1980) indicated that Black youth were in poorer health as young adults than when they were adolescents. Also reported were more instability and greater change in physical health among Black males than among Black females. Why is this so? Why have there been fewer improvements in the health status of Black Americans compared to White Americans in a society that has witnessed enormous medical and technological advances, and increases in the availability of medical services?

Attempts to understand the current physical health status of Black adolescents may be difficult because: (1) data on "normal" health changes during the successive life stages are sparse, resulting in limited knowledge of expected health changes for this subgroup: (2) studies often do not distinguish early adolescents from children and late adolescents from young adults; (3) Blacks are frequently included with other non-Whites; and (4) research on Blacks is often devoted to examination of specific diseases labeled as "Black-related" (e.g., hypertension, coronary heart disease, diabetes mellitus, elevated levels of cholesterol), with limited attention given to the individuals' overall health status or to the extent to which other illnesses and diseases (i.e., dermatological, allergic, eating, headaches, and dental disorders) associated with the physical health status of White youth also occur among Black youth. It may be also difficult to assess accurately the physical health status of Black adolescents because most studies fail to control for social class, geographic location, life-styles, and/or health behavior patterns. There is also an overreliance on low-income, clinical and/or convenient populations; and longitudinal studies that measure change and stability in Black adolescents' physical health are virtually absent. Finally, research designs are often unbalanced, comparing low income Blacks with middle-income Whites.

Given the aforementioned limitations, what can be concluded about the current physical health status of Black adolescents? Generally, researchers tend to focus in primarily three areas: (1) understanding the conditions (i.e., family health history, nutritional habits, economics, self-knowledge, and environmental factors associated with "Black-related" diseases) that are associated with poor physical health among Black adolescents; (2) clarifying existing relationships between predisposing factors in adolescence and the onset and progression of adulthood diseases; and (3) exploring the role of educational and medical systems in fostering declining health among Black adolescents.

Conditions and Precipitating Factors

Within group comparisons indicate no sex differences in the incidence or distribution of plasma cholesterol, high-density and low-density lipoprotein levels among Black adolescents, particularly those with a family history of heart disease, obesity and diabetes mellitus (Christensen et al., 1980; Durant et al., 1982). Other researchers suggest that physical exercise of Black adolescents resulted in high triglycerides and very low density lipoprotein cholesterol, thus lowering the individual's risk of the onset of hypertension and cardiovascular problems in adulthood (Durant et al., 1983). One study found that for Black adolescent males, suppression of anger was associated more with the incidence of hypertension than the individual's salt intake, or having a family history of hypertension (Johnson et al., 1987).

Studies comparing the physical health of Blacks and Whites further substantiate that Black adolescents are in poorer health than their White counterparts. According to Gordis et al. (1981) there has been an increase in the incidence of acute nonlymphocytic leukemia (ANLL) among Black children and adolescents of higher economic status that exceeds the rate of ANLL among Whites; however, incidence of acute lymphocytic leukemia (ALL) among Black and White children and adolescents has remained virtually unchanged. Although inconclusive, Gordis et al. suggest that the increase rate of ANLL among Blacks of higher socioeconomic status may be associated with increased exposure to cancer causing agents or other environmental factors related to improved living conditions for Blacks. Other racial comparisons of Black and White adolescent physical health status suggest that the low-density lipoprotein/high-density lipoprotein ratio among Blacks puts them at greater risk of experiencing hypertension as an adulthood illness than Whites (Frerichs et al., 1978).

Educational and Medical Systems

Investigations of the significance of education, or lack of it, in fostering poor health among Black adolescents indicate that Blacks were more knowledgeable than other ethnic groups about the transmission, treatment, and symptoms of gonorrhea and syphilis (Smith, 1988); however, they were less knowledgeable than White adolescents about the transmission and prevention of AIDS. Lower knowledge about AIDS was positively associated with Blacks perceiving themselves as having higher susceptibility to the disease than did Whites (Diclemente et al., 1988). According to Price et al. (1988) Black adolescents were also less knowledgeable than Whites about warning signs associated with cancer and were less likely to report intentions to take preventive actions to protect themselves against this disease.

Moreover, researchers suggest the need for increased health education to enhance awareness and to reduce high risk behavior patterns among Black adolescents (Price et al., 1988). There is also a need to identify linkages between physical health and personality factors among Blacks, and to conduct longitudinal studies that provide tracking information and data for making predictions of susceptibility (Christensen et al., 1980). Finally, there is a need for more equal access to health-care services and for health-care providers to become knowledgeable about Black families' health beliefs and practices in order to provide adequate care (Brunswick, 1980; Johnson et al., 1987; Smith, 1988)

Annotated References

Brunswick, A.F. (1980). Health stability and change: A study of urban youth. *American Journal of Public Health, 70,* 504-513.

A comprehensive investigation of the progress of health as measured by self-report morbidity data obtained from a representative sample of 536 urban Black youth was conducted. Data were collected at two points in the subjects' life cycle: age 12-17 years and age 18-23 years. Ninety-four percent of the original sample was located for the second period of data collection. The distributions of health problems at the two time periods were compared to measure stability and change. A greater number of health problems existed for subjects as young adults than as adolescents. More instability and greater change in health status were evidenced in males than in females. The single most prevalent health problem across the two time periods was gum and dental disease. Other problems included indigestion, musculoskeletal difficulties, gonorrhea, skin problems, headache, respiratory problems, and allergies. Overall, the symptoms and health problems increased significantly in young adulthood. Implications for future research are given as well as suggestions for health interventions.

Christensen, B., Glueck, C., Kwiterovic, P., Degroot, I., Chase, G., Heiss, G., Mowery, R., Tamir, I., and Rifkind, B. (1980). Plasma cholesterol and triglyceride distributions in 13,665 children and adolescents: The prevalence study of the Lipid Research Clinics program. *Pediatric Research, 14,* 194-202.

This Lipid Research Prevalence Study was a cross-sectional investigation of the distribution of plasma cholesterol and triglyceride levels in a sample of 13,665 Black and White children and adolescents ages 0 to 19 years. Data were collected upon the subjects' initial visit to the clinic. Findings indicate that Black males and females have higher levels of plasma cholesterol than their White counterparts; while White males and females have higher levels of triglycerides than Blacks. Regardless of race, levels of cholesterol and triglycerides are higher in females than in males. This sex-associated difference is attributed to the concentration of beta- and pre-beta-lipoproteins present in adolescent females. On the average, cholesterol values peak during pubescence and decline during adolescence across both races. Sampling procedures constrain the generalizability of these findings. They do, however, expand the available information on the complex relationship between age, race, and sex and plasma lipid distributions and suggest the need for longitudinal investigation of the role of elevated plasma lipids in children in predicting risk of coronary heart disease.

DiClemente, R.J., Boyer, C.B. and Morales, E.S. (1988). Minorities and AIDS: Knowledge, attitudes and misconceptions among Black and Latino adolescents. *American Journal of Public Health, 78*(1), 55-57.

To determine the extent to which knowledge, attitudes and beliefs about AIDS were associated with adolescents' perceived risk of contracting AIDS, a self-report questionnaire was administered to 261 White, 226 Black and 141 Latino students ages 14-18 years. Significant ethnic differences were found. Whites (71.7 percent) were shown to have a greater knowledge about the use of condoms as a method of lowering the risk of getting AIDS, compared to Black (59.9 percent) and Latino (58.3 percent) adolescents. Blacks' scores were twice as high as Whites' scores on the misconception category regarding casual contagion of AIDS. Among all ethnic groups studied, a lower level of knowledge was associated with subjects perceiving themselves as having a higher susceptibility to AIDS. The results from this study indicate the need for education about the prevention, contraction and spread of AIDS among all populations, but especially amongst certain Black and Latino adolescent populations.

DiClemente, R.J., Zorn, J., and Temoshok, L. (1986). Adolescents and AIDS: A survey of knowledge, attitudes and beliefs about AIDS in San Francisco. *American Journal of Public Health, 76*(12), 1443-1445.

High school students have been labeled as an at-risk population for AIDS because of the high level of sexually transmitted diseases among this population. Despite this fact, they have very low levels of knowledge about the disease. 1326 San Francisco youths (ages 14-18 years) representing several ethnic groups were sampled. Students responded to a questionnaire assessing their knowledge of the cause, transmission and treatment of AIDS. Ninety-two percent of those sampled recognized that sex with an AIDS infected individual was a way of contracting the disease, although only 60 percent knew the value of the condom as a preventive measure against AIDS. Students had very little correct information about the treatment of AIDS. A significant number (78.7 percent) expressed worry about contracting the disease. These results indicate the need for educational programs to enhance this population's knowledge on all aspects of the AIDS virus.

Durant, R.H., Linder, C.W., Harkess, J.W., and Gray, R.G. (1983). The relationship between physical activity and serum lipids and lipoproteins in Black children and adolescents. *Journal of Adolescent Health Care, 4,* 55-60.

This study examined the relationship between reported levels of physical activity of Black children and adolescents and their lipid and lipoprotein levels. The overall health of 53 Black males and 46 Black females (age range of 7-15 years) was assessed. The measures included level of high density lipoprotein cholesterol (HDL-C), reported levels of physical activity and a 24-hour dietary intake. There were no differences between males and females in lipid levels. A positive correlation was found between systolic blood pressure (SBP), total serum cholesterol (TSC) and low-density lipoprotein cholesterol (LDL-C) for Black children, ages 7-11 years ($n = 62$). HDL-C was negatively correlated with height and weight for those aged 12-15 yrs ($n = 37$) and was positively correlated with the number of sports that the adolescents played. Further, children who jogged regularly had higher levels of triglycerides and very low-density lipoprotein cholesterol than did children who did not jog. These particular findings suggest that regular activity among Black children and adolescents may positively affect serum lipid and lipoprotein levels. This relationship is particularly strong among adolescents, indicating the importance of habitual physical activity during the growth spurt years.

Durant, R.H., Linder C.W., Jay, S., Harkness, J.W., and Gray, R.G. (1982). The influence of a family history of CHD risk factors on serum lipoprotein levels in Black children and adolescents. *Journal of Adolescent Health Care, 3*(2), 75-81.

The present study evaluated the potential influence of family history of cardiovascular heart disease (CHD) and CHD risk behaviors on total serum cholesterol/high density lipoprotein (TChol/HDL) and low density lipoprotein/high density lipoprotein (LDL/HDL) ratios in a sample of Black children and adolescents (ages 7-15 years). It was hypothesized that those coming from a family background of heart disease, obesity and other related health problems would evidence significantly higher TChol/HDL and HDL/LDL ratios than those lacking such a history. Forty-four Black males and 40 Black females were given an overall health assessment and their parents completed a family health history. It was found that family history of stroke, diabetes mellitus and obesity appeared to significantly effect LDL/HDL and TChol/HDL levels. For example, the relationship between obesity and sex, obesity and age, and sex and age interactions pointed to significantly higher LDL/HDL and TChol/HDL ratios. Females, in particular, from a family background of obesity had higher LDL/HDL ratios. These effects were more pronounced in adolescents than in children, pointing to the need for early interventions to prevent family risk factors from having adverse effects on health, and more importantly, improve one's health throughout development.

Frerichs, R.R., Webber, L.S., Srinivasan, S.R., and Berenson, G.S. (1978). Relation of serum lipids and lipoproteins to obesity and sexual maturity in White and Black children. *American Journal of Epidemiology, 108*(6), 486-496.

This study examined 3,151 Black and White children and adolescents' (ages 5-14 years) levels of serum lipids and lipoproteins and assessed maturation and several other related variables. Lower cholesterol values were found in Whites than in Blacks. Regardless of race or sex, triglycerides, pre-beta-lipoprotein and beta-lipoprotein were positively correlated with body measures including height, weight and physical maturation. Alpha-lipoprotein, however, was negatively correlated with these measures. Except in White males bodily measures did not correlate with serum cholesterol. Obese children had higher levels of triglycerides, pre-beta-lipoprotein, beta-lipoprotein and had lower levels of alpha-protein than others in the group did. Although information obtained in this study comes from a single cross-section design, it is useful in explaining emerging patterns and relationships between body composition and maturity to risk factors which can set the groundwork for further longitudinal studies in this area.

Gordis, L., Szklo, M., Thompson, B., Kaplan, E., and Tonasaa, J.A. (1981). An apparent increase in the incidence of acute nonlymphocytic leukemia in Black children. *Cancer, 47,* 2763-2768.

A 15-year investigation of the incidence rates of acute leukemia (ALL) and acute nonlymphocytic leukemia (ANLL) was conducted on 286 patients ages 0-19 years living in the Baltimore, Maryland area. ALL type and socioeconomic and demographic data were obtained on each participant. Results indicate that, regardless of race or socioeconomic status, the incidence rates of ALL among all subjects remained virtually unchanged, in which ALL was three to four times higher in Whites than in Blacks. However, race and socioeconomic status differences were observed in the incidence rates of ANLL. Incidence rates of ANLL among Blacks of higher socioeconomic status exceeded the rates for Whites. Although inconclusive, these researchers suggest that this dramatic change in the incidence of ANLL in Blacks of higher social status may be due to increased exposure to leukemogenic agents (i.e. ionizingradiation) and drugs causing aplastic anemia, resulting from increased use of medical services. Moreover, the high rate of infections found among Black children of lower income may render protection against the development of leukemia. Hence, improved living conditions for Blacks of upper socioeconomic status and subsequent decline of infections may result in increased incidence of ANLL.

Johnson, E.H., Spielberger, C.D., Worden, T.J., and Jacobs, G.A. (1987). Emotional and familial determinants of elevated blood pressure in Black and White adolescents. *Journal of Psychosomatic Research, 31*(3), 287-300.

The purpose of this study was threefold: (1) to determine the relationship between elevated blood pressure and personality characteristics among adolescents; (2) to determine the influence of personality and other risk factors contributing to systolic and diastolic blood pressure readings; and, (3) to determine which aspects of experiences and expressions of anger best predict high blood pressure for adolescent males. Subjects included 219 Black adolescents and 279 White adolescents ages 15-17 years. A battery of inventories assessing personality characteristics and incidences of anxiety and anger expression were completed. Information about behavior, family background and diet was also obtained and measurements of height, weight, and blood pressure were taken. Findings indicated that both Blacks and Whites who reported frequently suppressing anger had higher systolic and diastolic blood pressure. Self-reports of anxiety and anger from Black males were both correlated with higher systolic and diastolic blood pressure readings. High anxiety of White males, however, resulted in high systolic blood pressure levels. Regardless of race, those whose parents had a history of hypertension had higher systolic and diastolic blood pressures than those with no family history of hypertension. In White males, systolic and diastolic blood pressure were associated with height, weight, and salt intake. Contrary to Whites, height, weight, and salt intake for Blacks were correlated with only diastolic blood pressure. It was determined that among Black males, emotional factors, such as suppressed anger, were associated more with high blood pressure than other traditional risk factors. In Whites, although anger was predictive of high systolic and diastolic blood pressure, more traditional risk factors, particularly weight, were the stronger predictor. The authors concluded that suppressed anger influences blood pressure by being a consistent pattern in one's life rather than a reaction to a specific instance. This suggests that interventions are needed to teach constructive ways of releasing anger, especially for Black males.

Klerman, L.V., Weitzman, M., Albert, J.J., Lamb, G.A., Kayne, H., Roth, K., Gerominini, L.R., and Cohen, L. (1987). Why adolescents do not attend school. The views of students and parents. *Journal of Adolescent Health Care, 8,* 425-430.

As part of a larger program designed to reduce absenteeism in Boston inner-city middle schools, this survey asked students and their parents what they believed to be the main reasons for students' absences. The sample included 544 students and 735 parents. The mean age of students was 15 years (range = 12-19 years). Sixty-six percent were from single-parent households and fifty-seven percent were of minority background (46 percent Black and 11 percent Hispanic). Findings indicated that approximately 57 percent of the students reported health-related reasons as being their primary reasons for missing school. These health problems included colds, headaches, menstrual cramps, and injuries. The other half gave nonhealth-related reasons such as dislike of school and teachers and missing the school bus. Twenty-five percent admitted they stayed at home to care for younger or older family members. One-half of parents responded that children were absent from school primarily due to health problems. Parents, more than students, reported that negative attitudes and emotional problems played a role in absence. Parents gave external reasons for absenteeism less frequently than did students. The results of this study indicate that there is a need for a multifaceted approach to the problems of absenteeism among this population. Several reported health-related problems may be eliminated through intervention, and if treated, would reduce unnecessary absenteeism. Nonhealth-related reasons, especially students' attitudes toward school, also require attention as they significantly contribute to the problem.

McLain, L.G. (1976). Hypertension in childhood: A review. *American Heart Journal, 92*(5), 634-647.

This is a comprehensive review which focuses on factors determining normal blood pressure and the incidence and epidemiology of essential hypertension in children. Information on the etiology, evaluation, and treatment of secondary hypertension is given. The author describes some of the difficulties and inaccuracies associated with blood pressure assessment in children and infants. For example, there is considerable disagreement and ambiguity among physicians as to a clear-cut line dividing normal blood pressure and hypertension in children. Essential hypertension is rare in children, as most are classified as having secondary hypertension. Familial factors, atherosclerosis, obesity, salt intake and race are some of the factors implicated as contributors to the incidence of essential hypertension in individuals. It is uncertain if hypertensive children develop essential hypertension as adults or if early treatment is effective in reducing the complications and mortality rate of hypertension in the adult population. Several articles are reviewed indicating a relatively strong relationship between early diagnosed hypertension and the incidence of serious complications and deaths from hypertension in adulthood. Controversy surrounds the issue of whether children having high blood pressure should be subject to extensive testing and evaluation within the hospital setting. According to some standards, children having mild high blood pressure conditions should have their diets and overall health closely monitored. Some physicians agree that when high blood pressure becomes a stabilized condition, antihypertensive treatment may be required. The need for longitudinal studies in this area to follow the progression and effects of treatment on hypertension from childhood to adulthood is recognized.

Miller, R.D. and Shekelle, R.B. (1976). Blood pressure in tenth-grade students: Results for Chicago Association Pediatric Heart Screening Project. *Circulation, 54*(6), 993-1000.

The Chicago Heart Association measured blood pressure in 13,321 tenth-grade students (ages 15 or 16 years at the time of screening) to test for occurrences of congenital and acquired heart disease. Measures of serum lipids, cholesterol, adiposity and cigarette smoking were also assessed as potential risk factors for these diseases. Data were analyzed with attention given to possible differences between subjects on such factors as sex, race, adiposity, pulse rate and father's educational attainment. Results indicate that systolic blood pressure was higher in males than in females, while diastolic blood pressure was lower in males than in females. This finding was attributed to the phenomenon of sexual maturation. Overall, systolic blood pressure was not significantly correlated with systolic blood pressure and correlated to a lesser degree with diastolic blood pressure. Among White males and females, father's educational attainment had a significant negative association with diastolic blood pressure. This was not true among Black students. Five percent of Black subjects had blood pressures that exceeded the upper limits of safe levels established by this association. The researchers acknowledged that the unrepresentative sample of Blacks may restrict the generalizability of the results to the wider population. These findings do suggest that future research should be devoted to determining the relationship between environmental factors and sexual maturation during the adolescent years and the incidence of elevated blood pressure during adolescence and adulthood. These individuals can then be targeted for prevention measures.

Nelson, D.B., Layde, M.M., and Chatton, T.B. (1982). Rubella susceptibility in inner-city adolescents: The effect of a school immunization law. *American Journal of Public Health, 72,* 710-713,

Using data from the Milwaukee Children's Hospital, this study sought to determine the impact of a "no immunization" "no school" law on the rubella susceptibility of 481 inner-city females (82 percent Black, 12 percent White and 6 percent Hispanic) ages 11-15 years. Comparisons were based on incidence of rubella before and after the immunization law was passed in the state of Wisconsin. Susceptibility rate decreased from 22 percent prior to the enactment of the law to 5 percent after its enactment. No significant difference was evidenced by race. Of those identified as susceptible, 90 percent kept their appointments for vaccinations. These authors concluded that enforced state immunization laws appears to be effective in lowering rubella susceptibility.

Nicklas, T., Frank, G., Webber, L., Zinkgraf, S., Cresanta, J., Gatewood, L., and Berenson, G. (1987). Racial contrasts in hemoglobin levels and dietary patterns related to hematopotesis in children: The Bogalusa Heart Study. *American Journal of Public Health, 77*(10), 1320-1323.

This study is a comparative analysis of racial differences in hemoglobin levels of a random sample of 100 Black and 220 White preadolescents (age 10 years) and adolescents (age 15 years) participating in the Bogalusa Heart Study. Relationships between hemoglobin concentration, iron, and seven dietary components associated with hematopietic activity were also examined. There was no significant gender difference in hemoglobin levels for pre-adolescents. Adolescent males had consistently higher levels of hemoglobin than adolescent females. Regardless of age or gender, Blacks had lower hemoglobin levels than Whites. Racial differences were also found in dietary components. Whites had higher levels of iron, copper, and zinc than Blacks. Even after controlling for variation in dietary patterns of both age groups, race still accounted for the greatest percentage of variance in hemoglobin concentration for preadolescents and adolescents. It is suggested that racial differences in hemoglobin levels will probably still exist even if Black preadolescents and adolescents intake specific "blood building" nutrients. Caution is given, however, to making any drastic amendments in the nutrition or health protocols of children and adolescents until the confounding effects of genetics and/or physiological issues are considered.

Phillips, S., Bohannon, W., and Heald, F. (1986). Teenagers' choices regarding the presence of family members during the examination of genitalia. *Journal of Adolescent Health Care, 7,* 245-249.

This study attempted to determine decisions made by adolescents when offered the opportunity to have family members present during a genitalia exam. The outcome of family members being present for doctor and patient is evaluated. Information from 1358 predominantly inner-city Blacks' first visit to a hospital clinic was recorded in which 550 patients were accompanied by a family member. Findings revealed that male and female young teens, ages 11-13, were most likely to be accompanied by family, followed by the middle teens (ages 14-16) while the oldest teens (ages 17-20) were the least likely to have a family member present. In general, males were accompanied more often than females, although this effect was only significant in the middle teen group. The majority of patients were accompanied by a female, usually their mother (71 percent). Younger people were more likely to be accompanied by a same-sex parent. In the majority of instances, the physicians described the presence of the family member as being beneficial to the patient. This raises the possibility, if tested among other larger, more representative populations, of making this a routine option for adolescents' genitalia examinations.

Pratt, J.A., Velez, R., Brender, J.D., and Manton, K.G. (1988). Racial differences in acute lymphocytic leukemia mortality and incidence trends. *Journal of Clinical Epidemiology, 41*(4), 367-371.

This study examined racial and mortality differences across time spans for Acute Lymphocytic Leukemia (ALL) occurrence among children. Previously, Whites were found to have a higher incidence of childhood leukemia, a disease most commonly seen in children before age 15. Results from this study indicate that, over time, this discrepancy between Whites and non-Whites was reduced and an equal rate of ALL mortality has become stabilized for both groups. Data from cancer surveys indicate that non-White children have lower incidence rates for ALL than do White children in the 3-5 year age group. Despite the development of chemotherapy, the ALL rate has remained stable among non-Whites. According to the authors, not knowing patients socioeconomic background factors, and bad prognosis, may account for the reported differences.

Price, J.H., Desmond, S.M., Wallace, M., Smith, D., and Stewart, P.M. (1988). Differences in Black and White adolescents' perceptions about cancer. *Journal of School Health, 58*(2), 66-70.

The purpose of this study was to determine if Black and White adolescents differed significantly in their knowledge and beliefs about cancer. Data were obtained from 573 Black and 297 White junior high and high school students (X age 14), using a modified version of the Health Belief Model. This instrument was selected because it measures multiple factors influencing respondents' attitude about and preventive actions taken toward particular illnesses, and it is considered a valid and reliable instrument to use with Black populations. Findings indicated that Blacks tend to seek medical care on a regular basis, whereas, Whites go *only* when they are sick. Significant differences between Blacks and Whites were also found in knowledge about the etiology of cancer, with Whites identifying more correct causes of cancer than Blacks. A larger number of Whites (76 percent) than Blacks (63 percent) identified several of the warning signs of cancer; yet, only one-half of all students, regardless of ethnicity, were able to correctly identify all of the warning signs as given by the American Cancer Society. More Whites than Blacks recognized several prevention measures. Whites were more likely to go to the doctor (28 percent) for a cancer check-up than Blacks (19 percent) were and also recognized the value of early detection and were more knowledgeable of treatments than were Blacks. Blacks were less likely than Whites to believe that they would develop cancer in their lifetime (44 percent vs. 37 percent, respectively). These results indicate a significant difference between Blacks and Whites with regard to many aspects of their knowledge of cancer. There is a need to educate all students, as there were large gaps in knowledge about cancer, in both the Black and White groups. Finally, due to several methodological and sampling problems, caution is warranted in generalizing these findings to wider populations.

Pumariega, A.J., Edwards, P., Mitchell, C., and Mitchell, C.B. (1984). Anorexia nervosa in Black adolescents. *Journal of American Academy of Child Psychiatry, 23*, 111-114.

Prior to this study only nine Black adolescents have been mentioned in the literature on anorexia nervosa. This report includes unique characteristics of two female patients, aged 15 and 17 years old, hospitalized at a university medical center for this illness. Although the patients were from different socioeconomic backgrounds (e.g., low-income and lower middle income), commonalities were evidenced in the following areas: (1) conflict about sexuality, particularly conception and pregnancy, (2) parental marital conflict leading to a separation, (3) conflict around "role" diffusion and enmeshment in the families, and (4) difficulty in engaging the families in treatment. Data from this report were compared to the paucity of literature on Black anorectics. Concern was expressed that nine of the eleven reported cases of anorexia nervosa in Black female patients occurred between 1982-1984, suggesting an increase in the incidence of this illness among Blacks. According to these researchers, the rising incidence may be attributed to increased use of the health care system in which such illness can be diagnosed and possibly evidence of Black females adopting values of the wider society regarding body weight, achievement, and control.

Rosen, J.C., and Gross, J. (1987). Prevalence of weight reducing and weight gaining in adolescent girls and boys. *Health Psychology, 6*(2), 131-147.

The cultural pressures on adolescent females in today's society to be thin are implicated in the rising number of adolescent females currently attempting to reduce their weight. This study provides additional information about adolescents' weight reducing and weight gaining patterns for the purpose of applying this knowledge in the development of safe weight and fitness programs. Weight modification strategies were examined to determine if some dieters are at risk of developing eating disorders or other detrimental eating patterns in later life. The geographically, economically and racially diverse sample included 1,071 White, 216 Black, 35 Asian, and 51 Hispanic high school students. Subjects responded to a questionnaire about dieting patterns and submitted a seven-day eating and exercise diary. Several statistically significant findings emerged. Females were four times more likely than males to be reducing weight. Males were three times as likely to be gaining weight. The four most frequently reported weight reduction strategies were exercise, decreasing calories, omitting snacks, and skipping meals. A small number of females reported using drastic measures to lose weight such as vomiting or appetite suppressants. White and Hispanic males and females were reducing weight more than Asians and Blacks. Black females and minority group males were attempting to gain weight more than White males and females and minority group females. The majority of females of high socioeconomic status were weight reducers while females of low socioeconomic status tended to be weight gainers. The majority of female weight reducers were underweight or of average weight. Male weight gainers, on the other hand, tended to fall in the normal weight range. These findings indicate a need for more comprehensive diet and exercise educational programs for adolescents about appropriate weight standards, as well as the information on the relationship of physical development during the teen years and change in body composition. Results strongly suggest that high school students are confused about what constitutes overweight and underweight.

Sallis, J.F., Dimsdale, J.E., and Caine, C. (1988). Invited review: Blood pressure reactivity in children. *Journal of Psychosomatic Research, 32*(1), 1-12.

This paper is an extensive review of 83 studies included in the pediatric literature on the rationale for studying blood pressure (BP) reactivity as a possible precursor of hypertension and coronary heart disease in children. The review includes a table summary of correlates of BP reactivity identified in 21 studies, with particular emphasis given to race, sex, age and stressors experienced by children. Methodological issues regarding assessment of BP and the reliability and generalizability of BP response to stress are discussed. Suggestions for future research and the use of BP reactivity assessments in clinical medicine are given.

Saxby, M.S., and Anderson, R. J. (1987). Dental cleanliness in a West Midlands population aged 14-19 years according to sex, ethnic origin and presence of 1 PPM fluoride in drinking water. *Community Dental Health, 4*, 107-115.

This study compared oral hygiene between sexes and ethnic groups and investigated the effects of fluoridated water on dental cleanliness. Peridontis information on 7,266 subjects between the ages of 14-20 years living in Birmingham and Coventry, England was collected. Based on the subjects' oral hygiene status, their teeth were labeled good, poor or fair. The water in Birmingham had been fluoridated in 1964 while water in Coventry was unfluoridated. Females in both locations studied had a larger number of teeth assessed as being good, with a smaller population being labeled fair. Blacks had a lower number of poor or fair assessments in both locations. Birmingham subjects had higher ratings of dental cleanliness across sex and ethnic groups. These results indicate the usefulness of fluoride as an aid in dental cleanliness. Future members of the targeted groups, indicated as having poorer oral hygiene, must be given more preventive attention. Although these findings are based on data obtained from an international sample, they may provide useful information for American youth regarding the possibility of fluoridated water causing an inhibitory effect on dental plaque.

Shear, C.L., Frerichs, R.R., Weinberg, R., and Berenson, G.S. (1978). Childhood sibling aggregation of coronary artery disease risk factor variables in a biracial community. *American Journal of Epidemiology, 107*(6), 522-528.

This study is an examination of the occurrence of aggregation of risk factors for coronary disease among 4,358 pediatric siblings, ages 2 to 18 years. Participants' anthropometric height, weight, skinfold measurements, serum lipid and lipoprotein levels were assessed. F-ratios obtained for all variables were statistically significant. All of the lipoprotein variables showed significant aggregation for the participants except alpha-lipoprotein, was not a significant aggregation for Black children. On any given variable, there were no significant different aggregation between Blacks and Whites where interracial analyses were conducted. The results of this study suggest further examination of the role of heredity and environment in the onset and progression of particular risk factors associated with coronary heart disease among family members.

Smith, L. Shoonover. (1988). Ethnic differences in knowledge of sexually transmitted diseases in North American Black and Mexican American migrant farmworkers. *Research in Nursing and Health, 11,* 51-58.

The purpose of this report was to determine the primary bases of knowledge of sexually transmitted diseases. A number of reasons exist to explain this fact, with one primary reason being the emphasis on acute versus preventive care among migrant farmworkers. North American Blacks and Mexican American migrant farmworkers' knowledge about the prevention, etiology, transmission, symptoms, treatments, and complications of syphilis and gonorrhea were assessed. Both ethnic groups (aged 18-35 years) had sixty participants. The total mean score on the sexually transmitted diseases questionnaire for both groups was a 13.53 correct out of a possible 22 correct. Age was not significant in predicting knowledge, but differences between ethnic groups did exist. Overall, the Black group had the greatest knowledge of sexually transmitted diseases. Sex and ethnic group interaction existed, with the difference in knowledge of the two groups being greater for females than for males across the majority of categories in the questionnaire. According to the authors, differences in knowledge level of sexually transmitted diseases may be due to differences in group members' lifestyles, cultures, and access to health care and education. There is evidence of a greater network among the Black population through which informal knowledge about sexually transmitted diseases can be passed. Further educational efforts and more widespread treatment of sexually transmitted diseases are indicated.

Wisser, L.S., Gittelsohn, A.M., Szklo, M., Starfield, B., and Mussman, M. (1988). Poverty, race and hospitalization for childhood asthma. *American Journal of Public Health, 78*(7), 777-783.

A four-year study was conducted to determine whether race and poverty are associated with rates of hospitalization for childhood asthma. Data were obtained from the Maryland Health Service Cost Review Commission on 4,896 Black and 4,145 White children ages 1 to 19 years. Results indicated that Blacks had a higher discharge rate across all age groups. Additionally, Blacks had a shorter mean length of stay in the hospital than Whites and were more likely to be admitted to the hospital in a situation defined as being an emergency. Black and White families having Medicaid status had higher discharge rates for asthma than non-enrolled families, and Medicaid Black children succeeded White Medicaid children in overall discharge rates. When studying discharge rates and their association to family socioeconomic level, it was found that both Blacks and Whites residing in poorer areas have higher discharge rates than those living in non-poor areas. When comparing the wealthiest White area with the poorest Black area, it was found that the asthma discharge rate was ten times as high for Black poor children. When controlling for Medicaid enrollment, findings revealed that increased asthma discharge rates were evidenced for both Blacks and Whites of lower socioeconomic status. These results suggest that, in general, Black children are very likely to be hospitalized for asthma, and are likely to be subjected to differential treatment. However, the incidence of early discharge appear to be more related to income level than to race. Additional research utilizing more accurate measures of income and health status among asthmatic children are necessary to clarify the relationship of poverty and race on the differential treatment of asthmatic children.

Other References

Brown, R.T., McIntosh, S.M., Seabolt, V.R., and Daniel, W.A., Jr. (1985). Iron status of adolescent female athletes. *Journal of Adolescent Health Care, 6*(5), 349-352.

Brunswick, A.F., Boyle, J.M., and Tarica, C. (1979). Who sees the doctor? A study of urban Black adolescents. *Social Science and Medicine, 13,* 45-56.

Farber, M.D., Kosky, M., and Kenney, T.R. (1985). Cooperative study of sickle cell disease: Demographic and socioeconomic characteristics of patients and families with sickle cell disease. *Journal of Chronic Disease, 38,* 495-505.

Harlan, W.R., Grillo, G.P., Cornoni-Huntley, J., and Leaverton, P.E. (1979). Secondary sex characteristics of boys 12 to 17 years of age: The U.S. Health Examination Survey. *Journal of Pediatrics, 95,* 293-297.

Hicks, E.J., Miller, G.D., and Horton, R. (1978). Prevalence of sickle cell trait and Hbc-trait in Blacks from low-socioeconomic conditions. *American Journal of Public Health, 68,* 1135-1137.

Johnston, F.E., and Mack, R.W. (1978). Obesity in urban Black adolescents of high and low relative weight at 1 year of age. *American Journal of Disease and Children, 132,* 862-864.

Jones, D.Y., Nesheim, M.C., and Habicht, J.P. (1985). Influences in child growth associated with poverty in the 1970s: An examination of HANES I and HANES II, cross-sectional U.S. national surveys. *American Journal of Clinical Nutrition, 42,* 714-724.

Jones, E.I. (1986). Closing the health gap for Blacks and other minorities. *Journal of National Medical Association, 78,* 485-488.

Kahn, H.S., and Bain, R.P. (1987). Vertex-corrected blood pressure in Black girls: Relations of obesity, glucose and actions. *Hypertension, 9,* 390-397.

Klein, J.R., and Litt, I.F. (1981). Epidemiology of adolescent dysmenorrhea. *Pediatrics, 68,* 661-664.

Leveson, I. (1979). Some policy implications of the relationship between health services and health. *Inquiry, 16,* 9-21.

Markides, K.S. (1983). Mortality among minority populations: A review of recent patterns and trends. *Public Health Report, 98,* 252-260.

Morgan, P.M., Murphy, R.F., Willis, R.A., Hubbard, D.W., and Norton, J.M. (1975). Dental health of Louisiana residents based on the ten-state nutrition survey. *Public Health Report, 90,* 173-178.

Orr, S.T., Miller, C.A., and James, S.A. (1984). Differences in use of health services by children according to race. Relative importance of cultural and system-related factors. *Medical Care, 22,* 848-853.

Parker, F.C., Croft, J.B., Supik, J.D., Webber, L.S., Hunter, S.M., and Berenson, G.S. (1986). Factors associated with adolescent participation in cardiovascular risk factor assessment program. *Journal of School Health, 56,* 23-28.

Pumariega, A.J., Edwards, P., and Mitchell, C.B. (1984). Anorexia nervosa in Black adolescents. *Journal of the American Academy of Child Psychiatry, 23*(1), January, 111-114.

Riggs, R.S., and Noland, M.P. (1984). Factors related to the health knowledge and health behavior of disadvantaged Black youth. *Journal of School Health, 54,* 431-434.

Silber, Thomas. (1984). Anorexia nervosa in Black adolescents. *Journal of the National Medical Association, 76*(1), January, 29-32.

Voors, A.W., Frank, G.C., Srinivasan, S.R., Webber, L.S., and Berenson, G.S. (1981). Hemoglobin levels and dietary iron in pubescent children in a biracial community. *Public Health Report, 96,* 45-49.

Wise, P.H., Kotelchuch, M., Wilson, M.L., and Mills, M. (1985). Race and socioeconomic disparities in childhood mortality in Boston. *New England Journal of Medicine, 313,* 360-366.

Drug Abuse

PATRICK C. MCKENRY
THE OHIO STATE UNIVERSITY

Summary

Although much research has been conducted on Black adolescent drug abuse, the literature generally suffers from conceptual and methodological weaknesses. Many studies are theoretically weak in both design and interpretation. For example, few studies deal theoretically with racial or cultural differences even when such differences in drug behaviors have been found; some studies even fail to specify race, and others group Blacks under a general category of non-White. Also, the literature generally assumes drug use and abuse among Black youth to exceed that of White youth. Drug abuse theories as a whole evidence a middle-class bias against minorities. A related assumption is that pathological characteristics of Black families are major factors in drug abuse among Black youth (Austin et al., 1977; Messolonghites, 1979; Tucker, 1985).

These invalid assumptions are maintained, in part, because of sampling bias. Studies have relied heavily on low-income, inner-city youth instead of sampling a broader cross-section that would include Blacks from middle-class settings and those from communities where drug abuse is not a major problem. Likewise, many studies have utilized Black youth in correctional or public drug treatment facilities where the level of drug abuse is greater than the norm. Because of a tendency to sample Black adolescents at greater risk, the focus of most studies has been on hard drug use by males. When low-income and/or institutionalized populations are studied without a comparison group or are compared with White middle-class adolescents, it is not surprising that assumptions of greater drug use among Black youth are supported. The failure to delineate carefully age parameters, coupled with the failure to compare various age cohorts of adolescents, has contributed to additional misconceptions. For example,when studies have examined specific age cohorts (e.g., younger adolescents), Black-White differences in drug use and abuse have been less marked (O'Donnell et al., 1976; Welte and Barnes, 1985).

Some recent publications have begun to overcome these conceptual and methodological weaknesses (e.g., Barnes and Welte, 1986; Brennen et al., 1986; Dembo et al., 1985). Future studies, in addition to addressing these weaknesses, must move beyond descriptive, correlational designs and deal specifically with causality; causal explanations thus far have relied primarily on retrospective interview techniques and causal modeling of culturally relevant and cross-sectional data instead of longitudinal designs. In addition, more in-depth investigations must be undertaken that are culturally grounded in appropriate health, sociological, and/or psychological theories.

What then can be concluded from this body of literature about Black youth and drug abuse? With the publication of more rigorous studies in recent years and the concurrence of findings from several studies, some tentative conclusions can be drawn. In terms of Black-White adolescent differences in drug use, there has been a general convergence in drug use, especially among younger age cohorts (e.g., Atkins et al., 1987; O'Donnell et al., 1976). While Black adolescents exceed White adolescents in use of cocaine, heroin, marijuana, and opiates, Black and White adolescents are very similar in the use of other drugs. It also appears that the etiology of drug abuse among Black youth can only be understood in cultural context. That is, Black adolescent drug abuse is probably best explained in terms of sociocultural factors, whereas White adolescent drug abuse appears to be most highly related to psychological factors (Dembo et al., 1985; Paton and Kandel, 1978). In recent studies of Black adolescent drug abuse, status incongruency and social stress theories appear to be strongly supported. For example, studies paradoxically have noted that high self-esteem, high level of adjustment, and generally positive level of functioning were directly related to Black adolescent drug use; the gap between high aspirations and low expectations appears to generate frustration and stress leading to "coping" by drug use (Gay, 1981; Paton and Kandel, 1978; Penk et al., 1981).

While drug abuse is widely recognized as a major health, social, and psychological problem among Black youth, intervention has focused on treatment instead of prevention and education. Findings from the research on drug abuse in the Black adolescent subculture have generally not been applied to service delivery systems on any level. Existing intervention efforts have tended to take the form of small-scale, local programs with targeted populations instead of addressing societal problems that underlie the patterns of drug use and abuse among Black youth.

Annotated References

Atkins, B.J., Klein, M.A., and Mosley, B. (1987). Black adolescents' attitudes toward and use of alcohol and other drugs. *International Journal of Addictions, 22,* 1201-1211.

Noting the little research attention given Black adolescent substance abuse, this study sought to identify the attitudes of Black adolescents toward these substances, the adolescents' level of use, and the extent of their participation in alternative activities. Forty-four Black students enrolled in alternative schools (grades 6-12) were administered surveys in their classrooms. The participants reported very negative attitudes toward drugs and extremely low levels of use of all substance categories assessed: tobacco, alcohol, marijuana, and other drugs (including inhalants, depressants, hallucinogens, stimulants, and cocaine). Attitudes were significantly related to the use of substances, and a significant negative relationship was found between involvement in entertainment and social activities and self-reported use of substances. The major implication drawn from these findings is that future research should focus on those factors that account for the dramatic increase in Black drug use after the high school years.

Austin, G.A., Johnson, B.D., Carroll, E.E., and Lettieri, D.J. (1977). *Drugs and minorities.* Rockville, Md.: National Institute on Drug Abuse.

The research literature on drug use and minorities is reviewed and critiqued. It is asserted that in spite of many well-designed empirical investigations on the topic, many suffer from the absence of theory and or bias in interpretation of findings. Another major problem is the reliance on institutionalized samples in which Blacks are overrepresented with generalizations made to wider society. Adolescents who are arrested or treated for drug use at public facilities are deemed nonrepresentative samples of both Black and White drug users. It is concluded that when all major studies are carefully reviewed, Whites have been at least as likely as Blacks and other minorities to be multiple drug users and to use all drugs, except heroin and cocaine. Also, racial differences in heroin and cocaine use have been declining among younger Blacks and Whites.

Barnes, G.M., and Welte, J.W. (1986). Patterns and predictors of alcohol use among 7-12th grade students in New York State. *Journal of Studies on Alcohol, 47,* 53-61.

This survey of 27,335 representative secondary school students in New York State found 71 percent to be drinkers and 13 percent heavy drinkers (i.e., drink at least once a week and typically consume five more drinks per occasion). Because of the large sample and ethnic diversity of New York, this study provided useful information on youthful drinking in various ethnic groups. In the subsample of over 3,000 Black youth, there was evidence of less drinking and less heavy drinking than among White youth. The authors speculate that these relatively low rates of drinking may be underestimates. Yet other studies of Black households in general have found less alcohol use by Black youth as compared to White adolescents. More in-depth research is needed to explain any difference in adolescent alcohol consumption.

Brennan, A.F., Walfish, S., and AuBuchon, P. (1986). Alcohol use and abuse in college students. I. A review of individual and personality correlates. *International Journal of the Addictions, 21,* 449-474. Alcohol use and abuse in college students. II. Social/environmental correlates, methodological issues, and implications for intervention. *International Journal of the Addictions, 21,* 475-493.

These two articles published together in the same issue systematically review and integrate the vast literature on the correlates of alcohol use and abuse in college students. While each article examines different sets of correlates, the second article theoretically integrates the findings of both reviews and analyzes salient methodological issues in the literature. Based on their review, the authors suggest that White, male Protestant/Catholics drink more than any other demographic group, and that this is less related to individual and personality variables than to membership in social demographic groups that condone and encourage drinking. The students who do not belong to this majority group, that is, females and Blacks, are not as susceptible to drinking, yet when they do drink heavily and abusively, it may be in response to other, more internal pressures, and therefore related to high levels of anxiety, neuroticism, depression, and low self-esteem.

Brook, J.S., Whiteman, M., and Gordon, A.S. (1982). Qualitative and quantitative aspects of adolescent drug use: Interplay of personality, family, and peer correlates. *Psychological Reports, 51,* 1151-1163.

The purpose of this study was to examine domains of personality, family, and peer variables and their relationship to the qualitative (stage) and quantitative (frequency) aspects of adolescents' drug use. This survey of Black ($n=245$) and White ($n=418$) high school freshmen and sophomores suggests that a mediational model best describes the *interplay* of personality, family, and peer in relation to the factors and the *frequency* of drug use by adolescents; that is, drug-prone personality and family conditions are associated with involvement in peer environments conducive to drug use. Yet each of these three domains was independently associated with the stage of adolescent drug use. The findings were similar in racial, sex, and social-class groups, supporting other studies that have found comparable psycho-social proneness to drug use among these demographic groupings.

Brunswick, A.F., and Tarica, C. (1974). Drinking and health: A study of urban Black adolescents. *Addictive Diseases: An International Journal, 1,* 21-42.

Interviews of 659 Black adolescents (ages 12-17 years of age) were conducted as part of a study of adolescent health in Harlem. The purpose of this phase of the study was to focus on health correlates of drinking. Major findings were: that drinking was regarded by the adolescents as a major health threat; that drinking increased with age, especially among boys; that drinkers, especially older girls and younger boys, were more likely to evidence health problems; that psychosomatic complaints were the most frequently cited health problems; that drinkers worried more than nondrinkers, but drinkers evidenced higher self-regard; that drinking was related to other lifestyle behaviors, notably smoking among boys and early pregnancy among girls, and anticipation of death by violent means; that drinkers and nondrinkers could not be distinguished by social class; and regression analysis indicated that drinking could best be explained by combination of lifestyle behaviors, psychosomatic conditions, and worry. It is suggested that adolescent drinking be recognized as symptomatic of other health problems. The authors conclude that Black adolescent drinking can best be explained as a means of coping with stress.

Brunswick, A.F. (1977). Health and drug behavior: A study of urban Black adolescents. *Addictive Diseases: An International Journal, 3,* 197-214.

Interviews were conducted with 752 adolescents (12-17 years-old) in a large inner-city and largely Black ghetto in the eastern United States. In contrast to the many studies of drug use, the data were collected from a community as compared to clinical populations and utilized personal interviews and medical examination to survey a wide range of health and health-related behaviors. Data analysis revealed that drug users smoked more than nonusers; received lower school grades; attended church less often; had poorer perceived emotional and physical health; more often were neither in school nor working; and more often aspired to a professional occupation yet evidencing a greater gap between aspirations and expectations. These correlates of drug use among Black youth are comparable to what others have found in studies among largely White and socioeconomically heterogeneous high school populations. The findings are also seen to be consistent with theories of status incongruency and social stress. Some younger versus older age differences were noted with the speculation made that different norms may be operating in different age groups.

Dawkins, R. L., and Dawkins, M.P. (1983). Alcohol use and delinquency among Black, White, and Hispanic adolescent offenders. *Adolescence, 18,* 799-809.

The relationship between drinking and criminal behavior was examined by administering questionnaires to 342 residents of a public juvenile facility. Analyses were performed separately for each racial subgroup, and indicated that drinking is strongly associated with minor juvenile offenses in each subgroup and strongly associated with serious offenses only for Blacks and Whites with other factors held constant. Relative to other background and behavioral factors, drinking is the strongest single predictor of criminal offenses among Black adolescents, yet of less importance as a predictor of criminal behavior in the other two racial subgroups.

Dembo, R., Schmeidler, J., Burgos, W., and Taylor, R. (1985). Environmental setting and early drug involvement among inner-city junior high school youths. *International Journal of the Addictions, 21,* 1239-1255.

This study sought to examine an hypothesized interaction between perceived toughness/drug use in their inner-city neighborhood and the adolescents' (1) demographic, (2) neighborhood orientation/ involvement, and (3) drug use context factors in regard to drug involvement. Questionnaires were administered to almost 1,000 students attending an inner-city junior high school. Most of the adolescents were Puerto Rican (43 percent) or Black (41 percent). The findings indicated that the predictors of drug involvement varied as a function of the perception of environmental setting, and that prosocial correlates of drug use were stressed in settings characterized by high toughness/drug use.

Gay, J.E. (1981). Alcohol and metropolitan Black teenagers. *Journal of Drug Education, 11,* 19-26.

Interviews were conducted with 728 Black youths (11-16 years of age) in Baltimore, Maryland to provide a comprehensive understanding of their health care needs. Twenty-four percent reported any drinking, and 15 percent were regular drinkers (at least one drink a week). Findings indicated that (1) both adolescent drinkers and nondrinkers generally recognized drinking and alcoholism as major health threats, (2) drinkers were more likely to report health problems, especially younger males and older females, (3) drinkers worried more than nondrinkers, yet drinkers evidenced higher self-esteem, and (4) drinking was related to other lifestyle behaviors and attitudes, notably smoking among males, early pregnancy among females, and anticipation of death by violent means. The author concludes that his findings support the view of adolescent drinking as a means of coping with stress.

Higgins, P.C., Albrecht, G.L., and Albrecht, M.H. (1977). Black-White adolescent drinking: The myth and the reality. *Social Problems, 25,* 215-222.

A stratified, random sample of 1,383 high school students in Atlanta, Georgia, completed a questionnaire on various aspects of adolescent behavior, including drug use. The data indicated that Black adolescents were no more likely and were often less likely than White adolescents to be involved in drinking behavior. Also, it was discovered that when Black adolescents drink, they are more likely than White adolescents to drink within the context of their family. The authors point out that the results cannot be explained by a "trade-off" in which Black adolescents substitute drugs for alcohol. The authors conclude that (1) Black adult problem drinking may not be as strongly related to adolescent drinking patterns as previously thought, and (2) Black adolescent problem drinking is not related to family pathology or disorganization as has been suggested by some authors; in fact, problem is significantly less than that of White adolescents because of family control.

Messolonghites, L. (1979). *Multicultural perspectives on drug abuse and its prevention.* Rockville, Md.: National Institute of Drug Abuse.

This monograph critiques the research on drug abuse in various American subcultural groupings. The author notes that a disproportionate number of studies of drug abuse among ethnic or minority groups have been concerned with drug use in Black communities. The large number of studies of drug use by Blacks includes many comparative studies, principally comparing Black and White patterns of heroin and marijuana use. Black drug use has become the "yardstick" for measuring relative degrees of use or abuse. Such studies can be faulted for failing to study Black communities where drug abuse is not a problem while relying on residents of ghettos and those in prisons, detoxification centers, and other environments that attest to arrest records. This focus on hard drug use among these groups is thought to have limited the range of drug abuse programs available to Black populations by emphasizing treatment rather than education and prevention.

Nobles, W.W. (1984). Alienation, human transformation, and adolescent drug use: Toward a reconceptualization of the problem. *Journal of Drug Issues, 10,* 243-252.

The author reviews the traditional conceptualization of adolescent drug use and puts forth a reconceptualization which holds that alcoholism and drug abuse can best be understood as embedded in the fundamental American cultural fabric as opposed to individual character flaws. American culture with its emphasis on individuality, separateness, and competition has produced a sense of alienation and frustration among its youth, and drug abuse is one symptom of this sense of meaninglessness. The solution to adolescent drug abuse requires the Africanization of America wherein fundamental societal values are changed to emphasize the unity and integration of human meaning and experience.

O'Donnell, J.A., Voss, H.L., Clayton, R.R., Slatin, G.T., and Room, R.G. (1976). *Young men and drugs: A nationwide survey.* Rockville, Md.: National Institute of Drug Abuse.

This national survey of drug use by young men (20-30 years of age) reveals some interesting Black-White comparisons. Blacks exceed Whites in current use of marijuana, heroin, opiates, and cocaine to an extent that suggests a real difference. Yet Whites exceed Blacks in use of alcohol, and Blacks and Whites are similar in use of other drugs. Younger Black and White cohorts reflect comparable use of most drugs, indicating a convergence in use among Blacks and Whites, especially for those drugs which Blacks currently use more than Whites.

Paton, S.M., and Kandel, D.B. (1978). Psychological factors and adolescent illicit drug use: Ethnicity and sex differences. *Adolescence, 13,* 187-198.

A random sample of 8,206 New York State public secondary school students was given a self-administered questionnaire to identify psychological factors related to illicit drug use. Two of four factors studied (i.e., depressive mood and normlessness) were directly related to illicit drug use. This association varied by sex and ethnicity, being consistently stronger among girls and among Whites. In addition, depressive mood was found inversely related to multiple drug use for Black and Puerto Rican males. These findings suggest that (1) psychological factors play a different role in adolescent drug involvement in various demographic and cultural groups, (2) sociocultural factors maybe more important determinants of drug use among Blacks and Puerto Ricans than psychological factors, and (3) sociocultural factors perhaps are more important predictors in minority groups than among Whites.

Penk, W.E., Robinowitz, R., Roberts, W.R., Dolan, M.P., and Atkins, H.G. (1981). MMPI differences of male Hispanic-American, Black and White heroin addicts. *Journal of Consulting and Clinical Psychology, 49,* 488-490.

This study surveyed first-admission male, young adult, heroin addicts in a Veterans Administration treatment program. Findings generated support for the hypothesis that better adjusted minority males are more likely than less well adjusted minority males to become addicted, whereas less well adjusted majority (White) males are more susceptible than better adjusted White males. It is contended that better adjusted minorities may be at higher risk because they are frustrated with fewer opportunities to actualize potentials, with some choosing a life of addiction which challenges traditional values and conventional life. By contrast, less adjusted Whites may be at greater risk because personal maladjustment interferes with their capacity to actualize potentials.

Tucker, M.A. (1985). U.S. ethnic minorities and drug abuse: An assessment of the science and practice. *International Journal of the Addictions, 20,* 1021-1047.

This thorough critique of methodological and intervention literature on ethnic minority "hard" drug use contends that despite the prevalence of "hard" drugs in minority communities and the unique patterns of drug abuse, there remains an absence of attention paid to special problems of substance abuse among ethnic minorities. The author notes that research and practice have become more enlightened over the last decade, due in part to a considerable increase in the amount of work produced by ethnic minorities themselves. The literature, however, still suffers from such weaknesses as: (1) the lack of etiological studies of ethnic variations in drug use patterns; (2) the lack of emphasis on the application of research findings to service delivery; and (3) the lack of drug use theories that account for the special circumstances of ethnic minorities. The author concludes that only massive federal support, through the implementation of minority-focused grants, can begin to address these deficiencies.

Welte, J.W., and Barnes, G.W. (1985). Alcohol: The gateway to other drug use among secondary-school students. *Journal of Youth and Adolescence, 14,* 487-498.

The "stepping-stone" theory of progression into drug use is examined, based on the alcohol and other drug use of 27,335 students from randomly selected public school districts and private schools in New York State. Rates of drug use varied substantially among ethnic groups with Blacks having relatively low rates except for marijuana. Alcohol was found to be by far the most common drug in all ethnic groups and always used if the adolescent used illicit drugs. The progression of drug use among Blacks, Whites, and Hispanics was in the following order: alcohol, marijuana, pills, and "hard" drugs. Among Blacks and Hispanics, pills were not as important a transition between marijuana and "hard" drugs as they were among Whites. Implications are drawn for drug and particularly alcohol education.

Other References

Anderson, W.H. (1983). TV and the black child: What black children say about the shows they watch. *Journal of Black Psychology, 9,* 27-42

Brunswick, A.F. (1980). Social meanings and developmental needs: Perspectives on Black youths' drug use. *Youth and Society, 11,* 449-473.

Brunswick, A.F., and Messeri, A.P. (1985). Timing of first drug treatment: A longitudinal study of urban Black youth. *Contemporary Drug Problems, 12,* 401-418.

Brook, J. S., Lukoff, I.F., and Whiteman, M. (1977). Correlates of adolescent marijuana use as related to age, sex, and ethnicity. *Yale Journal of Biology and Medicine, 50,* 383-390.

Brook, J., Lukoff, I.F., and Whiteman, M. (1977). Peer, family and personality domains as related to adolescents' drug behavior. *Psychological Reports, 3,* 1095-1102.

Cuffaro, S.T. (1979). A discriminant analysis of sociocultural, motivation, and personality differences among Black, Anglo, and Chicana female drug abusers in a medium security prison. *Dissertation Abstracts International, 39,* 4572B-4573B. (University Microfilms No. 7906217.)

Darby, C.A. (1985). *Smoking prevalence among Black and White males and females.* Washington, D.C.: Office of Smoking and Health.

Eisenthal, S., and Udin, H. (1972). Psychological factors associated with drug and alcohol usage among Neighborhood Youth Corps enrollees. *Developmental Psychology, 7,* 119-123.

Ensminger, M.E., Brown, C.H., and Kellam, S.G. (1982). Sex differences in antecedents of substance abuse among adolescents. *Journal of Social Issues, 38,* 25-42.

Gibbs, J. (1982). Psychosocial factors related to substance abuse among delinquent females: Implications for prevention and treatment. *American Journal of Orthopsychiatry, 52,* 261-271.

Jessor, R., and Jessor, S. (1973). *Problem drinking in youth: Personality, social, and behavioral antecedents and correlates.* Boulder: Institute of Behavioral Sciences, University of Colorado.

Myers, V., and Bates, J. M. (1974). *Youth, ethnicity, and drugs: Reports from the Job Corps.* Washington, D.C.: U.S. Department of Labor.

Rachel, J.V., Guess, L.L., Hubbard, R.L., Maisto, S.A., Cavanaugh, E.R., Waddell, R.L., and Benrud, C. (1980). *The extent and nature of adolescent alcohol and drug use: The 1974 and 1978 national sample studies.* Springfield, Va.: National Technical Information Service.

Zucker, R.A., and Harford, I.C. (1983). National study of adolescent drinking practices in 1980. *Journal of Studies of Alcohol, 44,* 974-985.

Suicide

PATRICK C. MCKENRY
THE OHIO STATE UNIVERSITY

Summary

Our understanding of Black adolescent suicidal behavior is rather limited due to the lack of research on this topic and the methodological weaknesses that characterize many of the existing studies. It is even difficult to determine the actual rate of suicide completions and suicide attempts among Black adolescents because: (1) The adolescent period is often not distinguished or is variably defined; (2) suicides and suicide attempts are sometimes not distinguished; (3) Blacks are often included with other non-Whites; and (4) Black suicide rates are thought to be grossly underreported for a variety of reasons. Attempts to understand the etiology of Black adolescent suicide behavior are made difficult by: (1) the failure to control for social class; (2) the use of culturally bound instrumentation; (3) the reliance on captive and/or clinical populations; (4) the lack of control or comparison groups; (5) the reliance on descriptive data; and (6) the use of "deficit" and other culturally biased theoretical models which superficially explain the dynamics of suicide among Black youth.

In spite of some inconsistencies, most data on Black adolescent suicide reveal an ever increasing rate of completed suicides and suicide attempts over the last thirty years, especially among males (Davis, 1979; Gibbs, 1989). For many years suicide was a relatively rare phenomenon in the Black community, but now adolescent and young adult suicides, especially male, approach, and in some reporting periods even exceed, the suicide attempt and completion levels of their White cohorts (Davis, 1979; Freedberg, 1986). (Because of the higher absolute rate of suicide completions and greater increase in suicidal behaviors among Black adolescent males, most studies have not closely examined the dynamics of suicidal behaviors of Black female adolescents.) Rates of Black adolescent suicidal behaviors would likely be even higher if more accurate reporting procedures, including better treatment facilities, existed in the Black community; also Black suicidal behaviors are often "masked" by drug abuse and violent behaviors (Gibbs, 1981; Seiden, 1970; Warhauser and Monk, 1978).

Various reasons have been identified to account for the increase in Black adolescent suicide rates in recent years. Both practitioners and researchers tend to place youthful suicide alongside other social indicators, such as drug abuse and unemployment, which have signified in recent years an overall decrease in well-being including a sense of estrangement or anomie (Gibbs, 1984; Freedberg, 1986, Kirk and Zucker, 1979). Much of the research has supported a frustration-aggression hypothesis and concluded that suicidal behaviors among Black youth are related to an increasing sense of disappointment and despair at continuing discrimination as Blacks progress closer to mainstream White society (Raskin et al., 1975; Seiden, 1981). Some see a breakdown in community structures, like the church and family, which have traditionally served as a buffer against stress for Black individuals (Freedberg, 1986; Spaights and Simpson, 1986). At the same time it is noted that professional psychological services have not increased to any meaningful extent in the Black community (Gibbs, 1984; Raskin et al., 1975). Still others, taking a cultural deficiency prospective, focus on the pressures, conflicts, and violence of urban life which lead to low self-esteem and sometimes self-hatred (Hendin, 1969; Kirk and Zucker, 1979). Finally, there are those that have concluded that Black and White suicidal behaviors have much the same etiology (e.g., Steele, 1977).

Implications suggested for intervention vary, much like the findings pertaining to the etiology of suicidal behavior among Black youth. Most authors, by specific recommendation or by implication, note the need for collaborative efforts among social service agencies, community organizations, and families (Gibbs, 1984) and the involvement of the Black community in program and policy development (Spaights and Simpson, 1986). Also, many cite the need for large-scale societal change to provide more opportunities for Black youth so that the gap between aspirations and expectations might be reduced (Freedberg, 1986). Some authors have suggested greater emphasis on a collective Black consciousness and pride as a strategy for directing anger and frustration in more constructive ways (Kirk and Zucker, 1979). In terms of treatment per se, it is clear that most Black youth are not receiving psychiatric treatment until after an attempt and then the quality of that treatment may not be comparable to what White youth receive. In addition, it is frequently recommended that mental health professionals become acquainted with the unique dynamics that underlie suicidal behavior among Black youth (Gibbs, 1989; Pederson et al., 1973).

Annotated References

Baker. F. M. (1984). Black suicide attempters in 1980: A preventive focus. *General Hospital Psychiatry, 6,* 131-137.

This study sought to determine from an emergency room (Yale-New Haven Hospital) sample of suicide attempters: (1) factors that could suggest preventive strategies; (2) any demographic change in the Black suicide attempter population in the 1980s; and (3) social support during hospitalization. The sample of 56 Black suicide attempters was composed of 17 males and 39 females and was predominantly (68 percent, $n=38$) adolescent or young adult (16-29 years of age). A psychiatric inventory was completed by interviewing each patient; data also included a retrospective medical review and a review of outpatient and clinical records documenting postattempt treatment. Based on clinical evaluation, preventive measures specified included: (1) education to improve stress management, (2) informational sessions for those with an emotionally disturbed family member, (3) removal of drugs from the environment of suicidal individuals, and (4) family crisis intervention at psychiatric hospitalization if the patient has not pursued treatment after two attempts. Compared to prior studies of Black suicide attempters, increased mental illness and a larger proportion of females were noted. Finally, it was discovered that family members tended to be aware of the stressors which affected the patient and tended to accompany the attempter to the hospital; thus family members were seen as important resources in developing crisis intervention strategies.

Children's Defense Fund. (1985). *Black and White children in America: Key facts.* Washington, D.C.: Children's Defense Fund.

Drawing on various government compiled data bases, Chapter 7, "Child Health," presents a demographic overview of the health status of children today. In terms of mortality, Black children are more likely to die than White children, yet older White adolescents have higher mortality rates than older Black adolescents because of their greater exposure to auto accidents and higher suicide rates; Black adolescents are more likely than White adolescents to die of homicide. Black adolescents (15-19 years of age) are less than half as likely as White adolescents to commit suicide. White male adolescents (15-19 years of age) are almost three times more likely than Black males to commit suicide. Most of the increase in adolescent (15-19 years of age) suicide between 1973 and 1980 is concentrated among White males. The White female rate slightly increased over this period, and the rates among Blacks actually decreased.

Davis, R. (1979). Black suicide in the seventies: Current trends. *Suicide and Life-Threatening Behavior, 9,* 131-140.

Studies are reviewed to indicate the increasing rate of suicide in the Black community especially among youth in recent years.The investigator found: (1) the suicide rate of 15-19 year old non-White females has exceeded that of their White female age peers; (2) the suicide rate of Black males, ages 20-24, has approximated and at times exceeded that of their White, male cohorts; (3) the suicide rate of Non-white males and females, ages 15-34, is now higher than it has been in 50 years; (4) Blacks between the ages of 15 and 24 commit suicide at a rate higher than any other Black age-cohort; (5) among Black Americans, suicide rates peak between ages 25 and 34. Contrary to popular belief, suicide is more of a male than female phenomena in the Black community as the rate of increase in suicide has been far greater among Black males than Black females. It is also observed that regionally Black suicide rates are the highest in the North and West and lowest in the South.

Freedberg, L. (January-February, 1986). For Black males suicide rates peak at prime of life. *Youth Law News, 7,* 13.

Various literature is reviewed with the conclusion reached that increasing suicide rates provide a graphic measure of despair among young Black men. In general, Blacks commit suicide far less than Whites. But for males in the 20-34 age group, suicide rates have risen dramatically in the last two decades and are now approaching the rates of White males in this age cohort. Black females, like White females, have rates much lower than their male counterparts. While the suicide rate of White male youth (20-24 years of age) doubled between 1960 and 1983, the suicide rate of Black male youth (20-24 years of age) tripled during the same period. It is also pointed out that the Black suicide rate peaks in young adulthood while that of Whites peak after age 65. The author accounts for the increasing rate of Black suicide in early adulthood by the disappointment and despair resulting from continuing discrimination as Blacks move closer to mainstream White society, what is termed a case of "false assimilation." It is not only hopelessness that accounts for the increasing suicide rate among Black youth, but also the erosion of traditional buffers (i.e., the family and the church) against the effects of poverty and exclusion. It is suggested that drawing on traditional supports and coping mechanisms can help Black youth cope during this transitional period when a large gap still exists between aspiration and opportunity.

Gibbs, J.T. (1984). Black adolescents and youth: An endangered species. *American Journal of Orthopsychiatry, 54,* 6-21.

This review of social indicators reveals that Black youth are relatively worse off in the 1980s than they were in 1960 in terms of rates of unemployment, delinquency, substance abuse, teenage pregnancy, and suicide. From 1960-1979, the suicide rate for Black males (15-24 years of age) increased three-fold and doubled for Black females in the same age group. Although suicide rates for Black youth are statistically still lower than that of Whites, it is suggested that the figures would be much higher (even higher than Whites) if the causes of death among Blacks were as reliably reported as are causes of death among Whites. The increasingly high rates of suicide among Black youth are explained by increased peer competition for college admission, jobs, and access to services – for which Blacks are in a disadvantaged position relative to Whites. Collaborative intervention efforts among social service agencies, community organizations, and parents are recommended in addition to a national policy for children and families.

Gibbs, J.T. (1981). Depression and suicidal behavior among delinquent females. *Journal of Youth and Adolescence, 10,* 159-167.

Forty-eight delinquent females aged 13-18 from San Francisco were evaluated for depressive symptomatology and suicidal behavior through self-report and reports from probations officers. Four out of five were found to be moderately to severely depressed; nearly one-half of the subjects had made one or more suicide attempts. In terms of depressive symptomatology, White subjects were significantly more likely to be moderately to severely depressed than were Black and Hispanic delinquents. While suicidal behavior was not significantly related to ethnicity and social class, there was a stronger tendency for White and middle-class delinquents to make suicidal attempts than non-White girls who were not middle class. The author concludes that depression in non-White delinquent females may be masked due to cultural restraints on affective expression of depression.

Gibbs, J.T. and Hines, A.M. (1989). Factors related to sex differences in suicidal behavior among Black youth: Implications for assessment and early intervention. *Journal of Adolescent Research, 4*(2), 152-172.

This review of literature on Black adolescent suicidal behavior has a four-fold purpose: (1) to analyze differences in patterns and rates of Black male and female suicide; (2) to discuss the validity and reliability of statistics on Black youth suicide; (3) to examine the limitations of three major conceptual perspectives on youth suicide (sociological, psychological, and ecological); and (4) to identify factors which contribute to gender differences in suicidal behaviors among Black youth. A major thrust of the paper is an examination of multiple external and internal stressors that impact on the lives of Black youth, making them vulnerable to depression and suicide. Selected factors in the context of developmental, family, school, peer, and community issues are examined to account for Black adolescent males' greater vulnerability to suicide relative to females. Implications are drawn for assessment, prevention, and intervention.

Gowitt, G.T., and Hanzlick, R.L. (1986). Suicide in Fulton County, Georgia (1975-1984). *Journal of Forensic Science, 31,* 1019-1038.

Demographic and trend analysis of 881 consecutive suicides among Blacks and Whites in Fulton County, Georgia is presented for the years 1975 through 1984. Of those victims 15 through 19 years of age, 47.7 percent were White males, 25 percent were White females, 20.5 percent were Black males, and 6.8 percent were Black females. Compared to the representation of this age group in the general population, White males were notably overrepresented, White females were slightly overrepresented, Black males slightly underrepresented, and Black females notably underrepresented. In trend analysis, White males and females at this age showed slightly upward trends; however, no trend was statistically significant. In the 20 to 24 year-old cohort, 49.2 percent were White males, 16.1 percent were White females, 25.4 percent were Black males, and 9.3 percent were Black females. In this age group, White males and Black males were overrepresented, and White females and Black females were underrepresented; White females were the only group to show a clearly increasing trend. The author concludes that contrary to other studies, these data would suggest that suicide among Black youth is not comparable to White rates; the authors note in their conclusion the fact that underreporting was minimized in this study.

Hendin, H. (1969). Black suicide. *Archives of General Psychiatry, 21,* 407-422.

This article summarizes data from the author's book, *Black Suicide.* These data on young adult suicides represent in-depth, psychoanalytic interviews with 25 male and female patients who had been hospitalized for attempted suicide. Five cases are presented in detail. Factors identified as being related to suicidal behaviors include the pressures and conflicts of urban life, violence in the family and community, and self-hatred. Suggestions for improving the mental health of young Blacks include Black pride movements which turn the young Black person's rage and anger outward toward societal change instead of inward toward self-destruction. Those Blacks who survive past the young adult years have typically made some accommodation with life—a compromise that has usually included a scaling down of aspirations.

Hendin, H. (1987). Youth Suicide: A psychosocial perspective. *Suicide and Life-Threatening Behavior, 17,* 151-165.

The psychosocial theoretical perspective presented here draws on the author's studies of suicide in various cultures and subcultures. This perspective also integrates data from a variety of disciplinary approaches in its analysis of (1) the relationship of violence to suicide; (2) parental socialization of self-destructive children; and (3) the direction of future research. In regard to Black youth, the author notes (1) that suicide is one of many stress-related reactions along with drug abuse delinquency, and crime; (2) the striking history of family and community violence; (3) the interrelationship of suicide and homicide; (4) the high degree of adolescent alienation from family by parental attitudes of resentment, hostility, and rejection; and (5) the need for in-depth case analysis of suicidal individuals as well as treatment modalities.

Kirk, A.R., and Zucker, R.A. (1979). Some sociopsychological factors in attempted suicide among urban Black males. *Suicide and Life-Threatening Behavior, 9,* 76-86.

This study sought to test three hypotheses relating to suicidal behavior among young, urban Black males: (1) Black consciousness and (2) group cohesiveness would be lower; and (3) depression would be higher among attempters as compared to nonattempters. Twenty Black males between the ages of 20-35 who had attempted suicide within a six-month period prior to the study were compared to a control group who had never attempted suicide nor had serious thoughts about suicide. The two groups were matched in terms of age, race, marital status, and level of education. Identification of the attempters was made by the Detroit, Michigan Department of Health; controls lived in the same general neighborhood as the attempters. A paper and pencil questionnaire containing several standardized instruments was administered to subjects in their homes. Findings revealed that the attempters evidenced less Black consciousness as hypothesized, but the hypotheses that the attempters would evidence lower group cohesiveness and higher depression levels were only partially supported. The authors conclude that the suicide attempt among Black males is a two-factor process involving greater alienation and lack of a positive identification as a Black individual. It is also noted that these findings may be specific to the era studied when Blacks were not yet assimilated into White American society and yet had been given the right and encouragement to do so.

McIntosh, J.L., and Santos, J.F. (1982). Changing patterns in methods of suicide by race and sex. *Suicide and Life-Threatening Behavior, 12,* 221-233.

Using data from *Vital Statistics of the United States and Mortality Statistics,* this study sought to determine changes in method of suicide by sex and race over a fifty-five year period (1923-1978). No age breakdown is given. Traditionally, males have used firearms and rarely used poisons, whereas females have used poisons far more frequently than firearms. Data analysis revealed that both White and Black males have increasingly used firearms over the years studied – both groups now using them in over 60 percent of completed suicides. The increase in the use of firearms is also quite apparent for White and Black women, more than doubling for both groups over the fifty-five year period; White women are still more likely to use poisons, but Black women since the 1950s have used firearms more than any other method. Possible explanations for the increase in firearm suicides among the sex race groupings include: increasing availability, ease of purchase, and growing acceptance of firearm ownership and familiarity. Very different patterns in methods of suicide were found for other racial groups studied, that is, Native-American and Asian-American.

Mercy, J.A., Tolsman, D.D., Smith, J.C., and Conn, J.M. (1984). Patterns of youth suicide in the United States. *Educational Horizons, 21,* 124-125.

Demographic trends in adolescent suicide rates are reviewed. It is noted that the U.S. suicide rate among youth (15-24) years of age has increased dramatically over the past 30 years – tripling from 1950-1980. The overall increase in the rate of youth suicide is due primarily to an increasing number and rate of suicide among young males. Ninety percent of young male suicides are White. Moreover, the White male group was the only race/sex category to show a clear upward trend in suicide rates from 1970-1980. Except for 1972, rates for young males of Black and other races remained lower than rates for young White males. Rates for young White females and for females of Black and other races were approximately equal and relatively stable over time.

Pederson, A.M., Awad, G.A., and Kindler (1973). Epidemiological differences between White and Nonwhite suicide attempters. *American Journal of Psychiatry, 130,* 1071-1976.

Using medical records of 1,345 suicide attempters over a three-year period, the authors attempted to determine differences in suicidal behaviors among Whites and non-Whites. The medical records were compiled by hospital personnel when the subjects were treated for a suicide attempt. Persons designated White (88 percent) included Caucasians, Puerto Ricans, and American Indians; non-Whites (12 percent) were almost all Black. Age race distinctions were not made. Major differences were found between Whites and non-Whites who attempted suicide. Compared to Whites, the non-Whites: (1) had three times the number of attempts; (2) had a higher ratio of women to men (6:1 compared to 3:1 among Whites); (3) were younger and of lower social class; (4) were more likely to be single; (5) were less likely to be diagnosed as having a psychotic disorder; and (6) less likely to commit suicide after an attempt. It is concluded that a different set of dynamics may underlie suicidal behavior in these two racial groups.

Raskin, A., Crook, T.H., and Herman, K.D. (1975). Psychiatric history and symptom differences in Black and White depressed inpatients. *Journal of Consulting and Clinical Psychology, 43,* 73-80

As part of a larger multihospital, collaborative study of drug treatment of depression, 159 Black patients were compared with 555 White patients on social, personality, and psychiatric history variables, as well as presenting symptoms. Racial differences in age, social class, and sex were statistically controlled. Patients ranged in age from 16-70. Findings indicated that both Black and White depressed patients were remarkably similar in presenting symptoms. Some differences did emerge on a number of hostility variables. There was a greater tendency toward negativism and introjection of anger in Blacks than in Whites. Also, depressed Black males indicated that they were more likely than White male counterparts to strike back, either verbally or physically, when they felt their rights were being violated. These two competing drives in Black males are thought to lead to much frustration and helplessness. Also a very high incidence of suicide threats or attempts was found among Black males. The clinical picture of the typical Black attempter emerged as a young male depressed as a result of personal dislocation or loss due to separation. High emotional disturbance is characterized by suicide attempts or threats to harm oneself or others, and generally goes untreated prior to hospitalization.

Seiden, R.H. (1970). We're driving young Blacks to suicide. *Psychology Today, 4,* 24-28.

A review of the incidence and etiology of suicide among young Blacks (focusing on males) is presented. The author's major contention is that the rates at which young Blacks kill themselves might be even higher than known if some homicides were included among them. In these "victim-precipitated" homicides, the victims seem to provoke others into killing them, often wielding guns or taunting others with threats of violence. These homicides are thought to be "masked" suicide because Black men perceive suicide as a weak and a "feminine" escape from problems; they define masculinity in terms of physical strength and toughness. Instead of giving into "cowardly" suicidal wishes, these young Blacks die, in their view, as heroes.

Seiden, R.H. (1981). Mellowing with age: Factors influencing the Nonwhite suicide rate. *International Journal of Aging and Human Development, 13,* 265-284.

Various demographic studies are reviewed to show a marked and consistent divergence in White and non-White suicide rates. White suicide rates increase with age, yet non-White suicide rates peak in young adult years and decline during middle and later years. However, non-White suicide rates are lower than those of Whites at all ages. Several hypotheses are advanced to explain the decline in suicide rates with age: (1) differential life expectancy – fewer non-Whites survive to the older years in which the risk of suicide is the greatest; (2) deviant burnout – reduced level of aspirations has a calming effect on youthful turbulence; (3) screening-out of the violence-prone – suicide and homicide are youth-related problems in non-White communities, and many potential suicides die by homicide (twice the rate of White youth); (4) role and status of elderly – elderly non-Whites are granted more purposeful roles and positive status than White elderly; (5) traditional values – non-Whites have more respect for age and stress the importance of survival; (6) age-specific motives – cultural pressure and unemployment selectively affect the younger members of the Black community more adversely. Implications include drawing on the traditional strengths of the Black community.

Spaights, E., and Simpson, G. (1986). Some unique causes of Black suicide. *Psychology: A Quarterly Journal of Human Behavior, 23*, 1-5.

This survey of recent literature attempts to identify some of the differences in the etiology of Black and White suicidal behaviors. While the discussion is of suicide in general, the focus is on adolescents and young adults where the suicide rate among Blacks is the highest. The authors examine such societal factors as the decline in Black group cohesiveness that has inadvertently evolved from increased opportunities for upward socioeconomic mobility. The authors note too the negative effects of persistent racial discrimination on the identity development of Black youth. Norms of (1) strict obedience to parents and (2) restriction of emotional expressiveness among Black males are cited as salient cultural factors. The lack of opportunities for positive social interaction in the Black community is linked to such self-destructive behaviors as drug use and gangs. The authors conclude by encouraging involvement of the Black community in the process of solving this problem, for example, educational awareness, development of public programs, and peer counseling.

Steele, R.E. (1977). Clinical comparison of Black and White suicide attempters. *Journal of Counseling and Clinical Psychology, 45*, 982-986.

Clinical evaluations were made of all suicide attempters aged 16 and over (n = 267) who presented at the Yale-New Haven Hospital for a suicide attempt during a one-year period. Clinical ratings by on-duty resident psychiatric residents consisted of 42 variables. Data analysis revealed few differences in Black and White profiles. The only significant differences were White individuals' greater use of suicide attempts to influence others, higher levels of depression, and greater deliberateness in planning the attempt. The author concludes that these findings counter theories that contend that the psychology of Black suicidal behavior is different from that of Whites.

Stein, M., Levy, J.J., and Glasberg, M. (1974). Separations in Black and White suicide attempters. *Archives of General Psychiatry, 31,* 815-821.

Childhood and antecedent separations were investigated by comparing White and Black suicide attempters with a matched (sex, age, race, and time of admission) control group of non-suicidal psychiatric patients. These young adult subjects were interviewed in depth, focusing on childhood separation (physical separation from a parent, parent surrogate, or sibling of six months or more duration from birth to 17 years of age) and antecedent separation (disruption of a close interpersonal relationship within one year of hospital admission or of the suicide attempt). The results of data analysis indicated that there were significantly more White male and female patients with a history of early childhood (birth to seven years), childhood (birth to 17 years), and antecedent separations in the suicide attempt groups than in the control groups. The Black female suicide attempters significantly differed from controls on both early childhood and childhood measures of separation, yet Black male attempters differed from controls in regard to early childhood and antecedent separations. It was not possible in this study to statistically compare the Black and White groups since the suicide attempters as a whole were not matched by race with the nonattempters. The authors conclude that while the data confirm the relationship of separation or loss to suicidal behavior, separation may indirectly affect mental health as indicating life stress in general and adverse interpersonal relations existing prior to the separation. In regard to Blacks per se, Black attempters and controls had twice as many childhood separations as did their White counterparts.

Warhauser, M.E., and Monk, M. (1978). Problems in suicide statistics for Whites and Blacks. *American Journal of Public Health, 68,* 383-388.

The accuracy of suicide statistics was assessed by comparing published health department suicide rates for an area of New York City with medical examiner records. Depending on the recording method used in a given year, Black suicides were underreported by as much as 82 percent and White suicides by 66 percent. Black suicides were more likely to be underestimated as a result of less complete histories obtained by investigating officials and greater use of jumping (as a method of suicide) where no note was obtained. The difficulty in assessing suicidal motivation and inconsistency of criteria used by various districts are cited as major factors contributing to the weakness of suicide statistics.

Other References

Bagley, C., and Greer, S. (1972). Black suicide: A report of 25 English cases and controls. *Journal of Social Psychology, 86,* 176-179.

Bedrosian, R.C., and Beck, Aaron, T. (1978). Premature conclusions regarding Black and White suicide attempters: a reply to Steel. *Journal of Consulting and Clinical Psychology, 46*(6), 1498-99.

Bettes, B.A., and Walker, E. (1986). Symptoms associated with suicidal behavior in childhood and adolescence. *Journal of Abnormal Child Psychology, 14,* 591-604.

Bush, J.A. (1976). Suicide and Blacks: A conceptual framework. *Suicide and Life Threatening Behavior, 6,* 216-222.

Bush, J.A. (1978). Similarities and differences in precipitating events between Black and Anglo suicide attempts. *Suicide and Life Threatening Behavior, 8,* 243-249.

Copeland, A.R. (1985). Teenage suicide: The five-year Metro Dade County experience from 1979 until 1983. *Forensic Science International, 28,* 27-33.

Davis, R. (1980). Black suicide and the relational system: Theoretical and empirical implications of communal and familial ties. *Research in Race and Ethnic Relations, 2,* 43-71.

Davis, R. (1980). Suicide among young Blacks: trend and perspectives. *Phylon, 41*(3), 223-229.

Davis, R., and Short, J.F. (1977). Dimensions of Black suicide: A theoretical model. *Suicide and Life-Threatening Behavior, 8,* 61-173.

Gibbs, J.T. (1988). The new morbidity: Homicide, suicide, accidents, and life-threatening behaviors. In J.T. Gibbs (Ed.), *Young, Black, and male in America: An endangered species.* Dover, MA: Auburn Hours.

Hendin, H. (1969). *Black Suicide.* New York: Basic Books.

Wylie, F. (1975). Suicide among Black families: a case study. In *Mental and physical health problems of Black women* (pp. 121-125). Washington, D.C.: Black Women's Community Development Foundation.

Academic Performance

SAUNDRA MURRAY NETTLES
THE JOHNS HOPKINS UNIVERSITY

Summary

Research on the academic performance of Black youth constitutes a relatively extensive body of literature. The methods used range from sophisticated analyses of data collected from national samples to modest explorations of a phenomenon observed within a single classroom. Likewise, conceptual foci are extremely varied. There are studies to determine the extent to which relationships found in majority populations can be generalized to Black or minority populations, studies to test theoretical formulations based on the realities Black youth face, and numerous studies that document the disproportionate representation of Black youth among those at risk of school failure and underachievement.

Despite the diversity of the literature three major foci may be identified. One focus is the educational environment and its influence on academic performance. In the 1960s and 1970s much of the literature reflected attempts to measure the impact of social experiments conducted in classrooms, schools, and communities. School desegregation was by far the most visible experiment, but attention was also focused on programs such as Upward Bound. According to Jones (1984), the gap in the achievement of Black and White students has narrowed in the years since such initiatives began. In the 1980s, however, researchers have begun to examine Catholic schooling and its positive effects on the performance of Black students (Hoffer, Greeley and Coleman, 1985; Keith and Page, 1985); the influence on intellectual effort of peer and self judgments about the appropriateness of academic striving in Black youth (Fordham, 1988); and how Black students perceive and are affected by stressors in the school environment. For example, in one study in a predominantly Black, inner-city intermediate school, students viewed general school disruption as the most frequent stressor, followed by academic problems and concerns (Grannis, Fahs and Bethea, 1988).

The second focus is psychosocial components and their relationship to performance. Studies of the self-concept of ability, internal versus external locus of control, and other aspects of personal efficacy have been of interest for two decades. Recent research has examined the role of attributional style; that is, a measure of the tendency to attribute outcomes on dimensions of internality-externality, stability-instability, and global specific (Belgrave, Johnson and Carey, 1985). Other investigations have examined the role of the family in fostering achievement behavior (Bowman and Howard, 1985), and attention has focused increasingly on noninstructional influences, such as athletics on student achievement (Braddock, 1981; Nettles, 1989).

Self-concept has been studied extensively and the results of longitudinal research, of which Hare's (1985) is illustrative, are being published. In view of the high attrition rates of and early parenthood among Black youth, Black adolescent girls and student dropouts are two populations whose characteristics and behavior have been of special interest to investigators. Among both groups, perceptions about the nature of economic opportunity figure in decisions these youth make about educational investments. In Felice's (1981) study, for example, students who had dropped out of school were more likely to view the occupational system as a closed opportunity structure than their counterparts who remained in school.

The third area includes research on the effects of programs to improve the educational outcomes of Black youth. Progress has been made in identifying approaches to higher achievement in the classroom. One family of methods is cooperative learning. As its name implies, students work together to learn materials the teacher has presented. Studies have documented the positive impact of cooperative learning in social studies and mathematics among Black ninth-graders and in middle-grade students in language arts (Slavin, 1989). Other innovations that might increase the success that Black youth experience in classrooms include incentive systems that provide feedback on student progress, multicultural curricular materials, and the introduction of critical thinking skills into the curriculum. One study (Nettles, Braddock and McPartland, 1989) is examining the effects of Touchstones, a project designed to stimulate critical thinking through discussion of texts from "great books" and other sources. The study has found that the discussions engage youth who participate least in the irregular classes.

Research is needed that focuses on developmental tasks of Black adolescents and how school and academic achievement impede or facilitate progress on such tasks. In view of the high rates of school dropout and poor performance on standardized measures of reading and mathematics among Black youth, research is also needed on effective strategies for remediation in basic skills and prevention of school failure and attrition. A related need is for research on the types and levels of incentives that have motivational significance for Black adolescents and the ways incentives must be structured to meet the needs of various subpopulations. Finally, studies designed to foster collaboration between practitioners and researchers should be undertaken. Such studies can be invaluable in efforts to identify gaps in knowledge about academic and other forms of achievement; to provide information useful in program design, planning and implementation; and to enhance the likelihood that research findings will be useful in practical settings.

Annotated References

Belgrave, F.Z., Johnson, R.S., and Carey, C. (1985). Attributional style and its relationship to self-esteem and academic performance in Black students. *Journal of Black Psychology, 11*(2), 49-56.

This study explored the relationship between attributional style and self-esteem and attributional style and academic performance. There were two samples. One was comprised of 46 high school students in the 10th, 11th, and 12th grades, and the other was composed of 43 students enrolled at the University of Virginia. Instruments included the Attributional Style Questionnaire, a measure of tendencies to attribute outcomes on three dimensions; that is, internal-external, stable-unstable, and global-specific; and the Rosenberg self-esteem scale. In both samples, an internal attributional style for negative events was associated with lower self-esteem. However, an internal attributional style for positive events was related to lower grade point averages.

Bowman, P.J., and Howard, C. (1985). Race-related socialization, motivation, and academic achievement: A study of Black youths in three-generation families. *Journal of the American Academy of Child Psychiatry, 24*(2), 134-141.

This study was designed to determine whether Black parents transmit to their children messages about racial status, whether such messages are differentially transmitted according to the child's gender, and whether race-related socialization affects personal efficacy or academic performance. Subjects were 377 Black youth aged 14 to 24 and members of the youngest cohort of a national, three-generation family sample. Measures included self-reports of school grades, a four-item index of personal efficacy, and two questions to tap race-related socialization themes transmitted by parents. Data were collected in 80-minute interviews. Subjects whose parents instilled awareness of racial barriers received higher grades. Orientation toward self-development was associated with a greater sense of personal efficacy.

Braddock, J.H. (1981). Race, athletics, and educational attainment: Dispelling the myths. *Youth and Society, 12*(3), 335-350.

This study examined the relationship of social class, academic aptitude and athletic participation to high grades, academic self-esteem, type of curriculum, college enrollment, college attainment, and educational plans in Black and White male adolescents. Data for the analysis were taken from the National Longitudinal Study conducted in the spring of 1972, with follow-ups in 1973, 1974, and 1976. The sample consisted of 1,369 Black males and 1,731 White males. Findings for Black males indicated that athletic participation was positively related to grades, academic self-esteem, college enrollment, college attainment, and college completion. These relationships were not substantially reduced when statistical controls for social class and academic aptitude were introduced.

Ford, D.S. (1985). Self-concept and perception of school atmosphere among urban junior high school students. *Journal of Negro Education, 54*(1), 82-88.

This survey assessed the relationship of self-concept to perception of school atmosphere to determine if sex differences existed in the two variables. Subjects were ninth graders – 53 males and 45 females, ages 14 to 17. All attended inner-city junior high schools. The measures included the Self-Observation Scales (SOS) and the School Atmosphere Questionnaire. Results indicated that more males than females scored high on the self-acceptance, self-security, self-assertion, and school affiliation subscales of the SOS, whereas more females than males scored high on the social confidence, peer affiliation, and teacher affiliation scales. Significant differences in perception of school atmosphere were found for students scoring low and high on the varied self-concept subscales.

Fordham, S. (1988). Racelessness as a factor in Black students' school success: Pragmatic strategy or pyrrhic victory? *Harvard Educational Review, 58*(1), 54-85.

The focus of this study was school success and its implications for the Black adolescent's relationship to the Black American cultural system and to the dominant society. The study was conducted over a two-year period in a high school in Washington, D.C. During the first year, observations of 33 students were made in the school and in community settings and in the second year, a 55-page questionnaire was administered to 600 students. A major finding was that high achieving students, especially girls, more closely identified with values of the dominant society than low achieving students and tended to adopt a raceless persona to maximize their chances of academic success.

Hare, B.R. (1985). Stability and change in self-perception and achievement among Black adolescents: A longitudinal study. *Journal of Black Psychology, 11*(2), 29-42.

This study examined the extent of stability and change in self-esteem, achievement orientation, self-concept of ability, and academic achievement among Black adolescents and among Black youth as compared to White youth. Subjects were 250 youth who initially participated in 1977 as fifth graders. Eighty percent were surveyed again in 1980. Measures included the Hare measure of general self-esteem and Hare subscales for school, peer, and home self-esteem; the seven-item Rosenberg self-esteem measure; Epps' achievement orientation scale, and math and reading scores on the Metropolitan Achievement Test. Results indicated that Black adolescents showed a pattern of positive instability, that is on over half of the measures subject scores were unstable, but the direction of change in group means was a positive one. The implications for hypotheses about Black adolescent development are discussed.

Hoffer, T., Greeley, A.M., and Coleman, J.S. (1985). Achievement growth in public and Catholic schools. *Sociology of Education, 58*(2), 74-97.

Earlier analyses of the differential impact of Catholic and public schools on the achievement of Black and Hispanic students and on that of the student population as a whole are extended to examine changes over the junior and senior years of high school. The samples were drawn from the High School and Beyond (HSB) sample and a variety of analytic techniques were used. The results indicated that Catholic schooling has a positive impact on growth in mathematics and verbal achievement, that size of the effect is greater among Black, Hispanic and lower-income students, and that the effects are due to course requirements (e.g., homework and number of academic courses).

Jones, L.V. (1984). White-Black achievement differences: The narrowing gap. *American Psychologist, 39*, 1207-1213.

This article presents evidence on the reduction in average differences in achievement between Black and White students. For example findings from the National Assessment of Education Progress (NAEP) on the reading performance of Black and White students at ages nine, thirteen, and seventeen indicated a decline in average performance differences at each age. Further evidence is presented from SAT data on verbal skills, and from NAPE and SAT data, as evidence of the narrowing gap in mathematical skills.

Keith, T.A., and Page, E.B. (1985). Do Catholic high schools improve minority student achievement? *American Educational Research Journal,* 22, 337-349.

This study compared the academic achievement of Black and Hispanic high school seniors enrolled in public schools with the achievement of their counterparts enrolled in Catholic schools. The sample was drawn from the first (1980) wave of the High School and Beyond (HBS) sample and included 3,552 Blacks and 3,146 Hispanics from public schools, and 370 Blacks and 485 Hispanics from Catholic schools. Factors examined in various path models were family background, school type, achievement (a summation of scores on reading and math tests administered to the HSB sample), and student ability, which Catholic schools often use as a criterion for selection. Results indicated that with student ability controlled, Catholic schooling produced a smaller effect on achievement than previous studies had revealed. Further analysis indicated that the impact of Catholic schooling may be attributed in part to more stringent curriculum.

Lee, C.C. (1984). An investigation of psychosocial variables related to academic success for rural Black adolescents. *Journal of Negro Education,* 53(4), 424-434.

The objective of this study was to examine the relationship between selected psychosocial variables and academic success in rural Black adolescents. Subjects were 110 students in grades eight to twelve. They completed a questionnaire comprised of seven scales: Family Life, School, Social Relationships, Activities-Interests, The Future, Morals-Attitudes, and Self-Concept. Reading and mathematics scores for each student on the California Achievement Test were obtained from the students' schools. Success in reading and math was related to nine school-related variables including realistic academic self-evaluations and study habits; eight family variables, including high degree of parental control and sense of responsibility; and seven variables pertaining to social relationships.

Lehn, T., Vladovic, R., and Michael, W.B. (1980). The short-term predictive validity of a standardized reading test and of scales reflecting six dimensions of academic self-concept relative to selected high school achievement criteria for four ethnic groups. *Educational and Psychological Measurement, 40,* 1017-1031.

This study had two objectives: (1) to determine the short-term predictive validity of the Comprehensive Test of Basic Skills (CTBS) reading score, sex, and six academic performance and (2) to determine whether an affective measure (on one or more of six self-concept scales) and a cognitive measure (CTBS reading) would provide a more valid prediction of grade point average than the cognitive measure alone. Subjects were 548 11th graders (274 males, 274 females; 292 Anglos, 28 Asians, 38 Blacks and 190 Latinos). Intercorrelations of all variables were computed, and stepwise multiple regression analyses were conducted to determine the correlation between grade point average and optimally weighted combinations of predictor variables.

Nettles, S.M. (1989). The role of community involvement in fostering investment behavior in low-income Black adolescents: A theoretical perspective. *Journal of Adolescent Research, 4*(2), 190-201.

In this article a framework for studying community actions to improve the status of low-income Black adolescents is presented. The framework identifies processes predominant in community activities and differentiates them according to content, frequency and relation of outcome and process. Further, the processes are linked to the outcomes expected for youth who participate in community programs and to research methods for examining the outcomes. Investment behavior is described as one outcome that may be particularly amenable to community action, with theoretical significance to achievement outcomes.

Slavin, R.E. (1989). Cooperative learning and student achievement. In R.E. Slavin (Ed.). *School and Classroom Organization.* Hillsdale, N.J.: Lawrence Erlbaum.

This article presents a comprehensive review of evidence on the effectiveness of cooperative learning on student achievement. The major approaches to cooperative learning (for example, student team learning as developed by Slavin and his associates at the Johns Hopkins University) are described and findings from sixty studies are analyzed. Studies on Black populations in the United States and Nigeria showed significant effects for cooperative learning across groups who varied in age, grade, and academic subject.

Other References

Allen, W.R. (1978). Race, family setting and adolescent achievement orientation. *Journal of Negro Education, 47*(3), 230-243.

Bond, L. (1989). The effects of special preparation on measures of scholastic ability. In R.L. Linn (Ed.) *Educational Measurement.* New York: American Council on Education.

Coleman, J.S., Campbell, E., Hobson, E., McFarland, J., Mood, A., Weinfeld, F., and York, R. (1966). *Equality of educational opportunity.* Washington, D.C.: U.S. Government Printing Office.

Council of Chief State School Officers (1988). *School success for students at risk: Analysis and recommendations of the Council of Chief State School Officers.* Orlando: Harcourt Brace Jovanovich.

Epps, E. (Ed.). (1969). Motivation and academic achievement of the Negro American (special issue). *Journal of Social Issues, 25*(3).

Felice, L.G. (1981). Black student dropout behavior: Disengagement from school rejection and racial discrimination. *Journal of Negro Education, 50*(4), 415-424.

Fordham, S., and Ogbu, J. (1986). Black students' school success: Coping with the "burden of acting White." *The Urban Review, 18*(3), 176-206.

Fry, P.S., and Coe, K.J. (1980). Achievement performance of internally and externally oriented Black and White high school students under conditions of competition and co-operation expectancies. *British Journal of Education Psychology, 50,* 162-167.

Fulkerson, K.F., Furr, S., and Brown, D. (1983). Expectations and achievement among third-, sixth-, and ninth-grade Black and White males and females. *Developmental Psychology, 19*(2), 231-236.

Grannis, J.C., Fahs, M.E., and Bethea, W.L. (1988). *Project on academic striving: The moderation of stress in the lives of the students of an urban intermediate school: A project to coordinate research and environmental intervention.* New York: Public Education Association.

Gurin, P., and Epps, E. (1975). *Black consciousness, identity, and achievement: A study of students in historically Black colleges.* New York: John Wiley.

Hare, B. (1979). *Black girls: A comparative analysis of self-perception and achievement by race, sex and socioeconomic background.* (Rep. No. 271.) Baltimore, Md.: Johns Hopkins University, Center for Social Organization of Schools.

Jacobowitz, T. (1983). Relationship of sex, achievement and science self-concept to the science career preferences of Black students. *Journal of Research in Science Teaching, 20,* 621-628.

Jacobson, C.K. (1978). The effects of student performance and racial attitudes on self-depreciation in biracial groups. *International Journal of Group Tensions, 9,* 201-210.

Johnson, S.T. (1984). *Preparing Black students for the SAT–does it make a difference? An evaluation report of the NAACP Test Preparation Project.*

New York: National Association for the Advancement of Colored People. (ERIC Document Reproduction Service No. ED 247 350.)

Laffey, J.M. (1982). The assessment of involvement with school students. *Journal of Educational Psychology, 74*(1), 62-71.

Minatoya, L., and Sedlacek, W.E. (1983). Assessing differential needs among university freshman: A comparison among racial/ethnic subgroups. *Journal of Non-White Concerns in Personnel and Guidance, 11*(4), 126-132.

Murray, S.R., et al. (1982). *National Evaluation of the PUSH for Excellence Project: Final Report.* Washington, D.C.: American Institutes for Research. (ERIC Document Reproduction Service No. ED 240 225.)

Nettles, S.M., Braddock, J.H., and McPartland, J.M. (1989). *Evaluation of classroom instruction experiment for active learning and higher order thinking in the middle grades.* Paper presented at the annual meeting of the American Educational Research Association, San Francisco. (March.)

Powell, G.J. (1985). Self-concepts among Afro-American students in racially isolated minority schools: Some regional differences. *Journal of the American Academy of Child Psychiatry, 24*(2), 142-149.

Schweinhart, L.J., and Weikart, D.P. (1980). *Young children grow up: The effects of the Perry Preschool Program on youth through age fifteen.* Ypsilanti, Mich.: The High/Scope Educational Foundation.

Simmons, R., Brown, L., Mitsch, D., and Blyth, D. (1978). Self-esteem and achievement of Black and White adolescents. *Social Problems, 26*(1), 7-16.

Simmons, W. (1979). The relationship between academic status and future expectations among low-income Blacks. *Journal of Black Psychology, 6*(1), 7-16.

Slaughter, D.T., and Epps, E.G. (Eds.) (1987). The Black child's home environment and student achievement (Special Issue.) *Journal of Negro Education, 56*(1).

Slaughter, D.T., and Schneider, B. (1986). *Newcomers: Blacks in private schools* (Final report). Washington, D.C.: National Institute of Education.

Slavin, R.E. (1987). Cooperative learning and the achievement of disadvantaged students. In D. Strickland and E.J. Cooper (Eds.) *Educating Black Children.* Washington: Howard University.

Smith, E. (1982). The Black female adolescent: A review of the educational, career, and psychological literature. *Psychology of Women Quarterly,* *6*(3), 261-288.

Trent, W.T. and McPartland, J.M. (1982). *The sense of well-being and opportunity of America's youth: Some sources of race and sex differences in early adolescence.* Baltimore: The Johns Hopkins University. (ERIC Document Reproduction Service No. ED 242 798.)

Education and Occupational Choice

CAROL J. CARTER
NORTHEASTERN UNIVERSITY

Summary

Adolescence is a transitory stage in human development between childhood and adulthood. Research on Black adolescent youth is limited in focus, however, generally concentrating on maladaptive social behaviors (Gibbs, 1985) and neglecting the experiences of Black female adolescents altogether. This summary will review research on significant factors that influence the educational attainment of Black adolescents by assessing the learning environment and the occupational choices of this group. Particular attention is directed to Black adolescent females, as this is the chapter author's primary research interest.

The Learning Environment

The learning environment is a significant influence in the academic achievement and the intellectual development of students. Three components of that environment serve as the focus of this summary: teacher role, the type of school, and racial attitudes.

Studies of the relationship between teacher expectation and student performance substantiate the theory that teacher expectation influences student performance and academic development (Baron, Tom, and Cooper, 1985; Lightfoot, 1976; Rosenthal and Jacobson, 1968). There is also evidence that teacher expectation can influences student performance along gender lines (Cornbleth and Korth, 1980; DeBord, Griffin and Clark, 1977; Simons, 1980).

Examinations of teacher perceptions of students further substantiate the teacher's power in the classroom. For example, a study by Pollard (1979) indicates that White female students were evaluated by teachers as "better" than all other students. Washington (1982) reports that Black teachers in desegregated classrooms were generally more critical of Black female students, and White teachers in similar classrooms were more critical of White male students. Grant (1984) notes that teachers perceived Black females as socially mature but not as academically competent as their White counterparts. Though the literature does not link conclusively the relationship between teachers' perceptions and the educational development of Black adolescents, it does suggest serious difficulty in the interaction between teachers and students when teachers hold a negative perception of pupils.

The research on teacher attitude documents the resulting impact on student retention. Timberlake (1981) studied a group of high school Black females identified as "high risk" students and found that those defined as persisters generally had a more positive attitude about schooling than nonpersisters. Such positive attitudes were attributed to the amount of concern teachers demonstrated. Conversely, the lack of teacher concern was identified as a factor among nonpersisters.

Research on secondary school characteristics such as racial composition and curricular focus show that these may have gender-biased impact on the educational experiences of Black adolescents. Chester (1983) studied two types of high schools and found that Black females expressed lower career aspirations and less relevant vocational interest in a liberal arts school than those Black females enrolled in a vocational school. He indicates that race and gender are significant factors in the performance of the females. Crain, Mahard, and Narot (1982) documented that in secondary schools where the "climate" was unfavorable to Blacks, the academic performance of Black females was reduced. Black males, however, were not as adversely affected in these schools.

Racial climate is another significant factor in the academic achievement and intellectual development of Black students. Studies of desegregated classrooms indicate that Black females feel more socially isolated than their Black or White peers. While academic achievement among Black students is lower than among White students in the same class setting, Crain, Mahard and Narot (1982), and Hare (1979) report that Black females exhibit higher academic achievement than their Black male counterparts. Several researchers have also found Black female students possess highly developed interpersonal skills in their interactions with both Black and White peers and teachers (Crain, Mahard and Narot, 1982; Grant, 1984; Scott-Jones and Clark, 1986). As a group Black female students are also less likely than their White or Black peers to be intimidated by verbal or physical aggression; they demonstrate more of an egalitarian attitude than other students.

Career Development and Education

The level of education one attains influences the kind of career or occupational opportunities available in American society. Much of the literature on occupational development among Black youth is based on studies of college students and adult populations (Burlew, 1978; Gurin and Gaylord, 1976). A major reason for this focus on adults is a presumed level of maturity and the belief that a more adult population understands work values more than adolescents (Smith, 1982).

Research on the occupational concerns of Black females concentrates primarily on related employment or work issues. Murray (1985) argued that studies on the work experience of Black female adolescents can be grouped into four categories: the sex-role of occupational choices (e.g., Hall, 1973; Winters and Frankel, 1984); rates of participation by Black teenaged girls in the labor force (e.g., Wallace, Datcher, and Malveaux, 1980); the effects of teenaged nonemployment on the subsequent success in the labor market (e.g., Corcoran, 1980); and the inadequacy of Black girls' preparation for work (e.g., Roderick and Davis, 1973).

Additional studies on career development show that adolescent Black females exhibit comparable or higher educational or career aspirations than their White cohorts (Allen, 1979; George, 1981; Hare, 1979). Other works reveal that Black females appear less able to focus on attaining their expectations than other groups (Allen, 1978; Dillard and Perrin, 1980; Murray, 1985; Winters and Frankel, 1984).

Although the experiences of Black women in American society validate the realization that work will be an integral part of their lives, the research substantiates that many of the educational experiences of Black female adolescents do not provide them with the requisite skills for career planning. Adolescent Black females appear to be inhibited by many factors, including: fear of success, inability to set realistic career goals and aspirations, low socioeconomic status, and few role models.

Annotated References

Allen, W. (1979). Family roles, occupational statuses, and achievement orientations among Black women in the United States. *Signs: Journal of Women in Culture and Society, 4,* 670-686.

    This article discusses the status of Black females in the labor force by comparing their occupational status and achievement orientation. Data were used from a national longitudinal study of 21,000 high school seniors during the period of 1964-1974. Results indicate that many Black females had shifted in employment from service work to white-collar positions. Educational aspirational levels were higher among Black than among White females.

Carter, C.J. (1988). Black female students: Issues and considerations for teachers of teachers. *Educational Considerations, 15*(1), 31-36.

This article is a review of the literature of teachers' attitudes, expectations and perceptions of Black female students. The research reveals that Black female students are ignored as a unique population. An analysis of their status has broad implications for the educational development of Black females and for educators who prepare teacher candidates. In response to this omission in teacher education programs, several recommendations are offered to teacher educators to improve the educational well-being of Black female students.

Chester, N. (1983). Sex differentiation in two high school environments: Implications for career development among Black adolescent females. *Journal of Social Issues, 39*(3) 29-40.

This is a report of a comparative study of 127 Black males and females on career-related variables at two high schools; one a predominately White liberal arts school and the other an integrated vocational high school. The hypotheses were that sex differences exist among Black students in each of the schools and that sex differences would favor males. These hypotheses were confirmed. One of the recommendations was that additional studies based on gender differentiations be done to assess group behavior, particularly on Black females.

Clark, M.L. (1986, April). The status of interethnic contact and ethnocentrism among White, Hispanic, and Black students. Paper presented at the American Educational Research Association, San Francisco, Calif.

This report analyzed social interactive patterns to assess interracial contact, acceptance and dating practices among the Black, Hispanic and White racial groups. The results showed that all the ethnic groups preferred within-race friendships. However, if friendships are initiated across racial line, in White majority settings, they were initiated more often by minority students. Within desegregated schools, resegregation occurred among all students. Interracial dating occurred more frequently among all males than among Black and Hispanic females. The author noted that planned learning activities facilitated interracial interactions.

Doughty, R.N., and Doughty, J.J. (1984). Toward a meaningful education for Black girls: Perspectives from two policy makers. *SAGE: A Scholarly Journal on Black Women, 1*(1), 12-13.

This article is based upon the responses of two policy-makers, a school superintendent and a staff development specialist, as part of the Black Women's Educational Policy and Research Network Project which was held in San Francisco during March 1981. The authors explore three areas related to these issues by: (1) identifying the needs of Black girls, (2) recommending program initiatives to address the stated needs, and (3) defining the role of school personnel to foster these efforts in educational systems. The authors provide several strategies that will enable educators to be in the vanguard of movements to achieve equity in public schools.

George, V.D. (1981). *Occupational aspirations of talented adolescent females.* Paper presented at the meeting of the Association for Women in Psychology, Boston, Mass.

George compares career aspirational levels of Black and White girls. The results indicate that Black subjects had high aspirational levels. White subjects did not differ from Blacks in their aspiration levels; however, they had a lower incidence of fear of success than Black adolescents. The study suggests that socioeconomic factors exert a strong influence on subject responses.

Grant, L. (1984). Black females' "place" in desegregated classrooms. *Sociology of Education, 5*(2), 98-111.

This is an ethnographic study of observations of students and interviews with teachers in first grade desegregated classrooms. The author uses qualitative analysis of the classroom to assess teachers' behaviors and attitudes towards students to determine their impact upon the roles of children within their social configurations. The findings show that Black girls are treated differently from other students in classrooms. The broad implication of the study is that the desegregated classroom contributes to the socialization of Black females by guiding them toward stereotypical roles and functions as defined by the larger society, thereby establishing their "place."

Hare, B.R. (1979). *Black girls: A comparative analysis of self-perception and achievement by race, sex and socioeconomic background.* (Report No. 271.) Baltimore, Md.: Johns Hopkins University, Center for Social Organization of schools.

This is a report of comparisons of self-esteem and academic achievement among fifth grade Black and White students. The findings indicate that Black girls occupy a psychological and academic middle ground when compared with other groups. For example, White girls had higher reading and math test scores than Black girls, but Black girls scored higher than Black boys. Black boys scored higher on the nonacademic categories. Hare concludes that further study on gender difference among Black children is needed.

Lightfoot, S.L. (1976). Socialization and education of young Black girls in school. *Teachers College Record,* 78(2), 239-262.

This article reviews the influences in the socialization of Black girls. Two major sources for learning about the educational experiences of Black girls are identified: (1) literature on teacher's relationship with young Black girls and (2) literature on teacher's reactions to Black children in the classroom. The author suggests that explorations beyond the classroom be considered in analyzing the behaviors and the socialization of Black girls.

Miller, R.L. (1989). Desegregation experiences of minority students: Adolescent coping strategies in five Connecticut high schools. *Journal of Adolescent Research,* 4(2), 173-190.

This study examines the adolescent subculture of minority students in desegregated learning environments. It is based upon the experiences of 69 participants in the bussing program entitled, Project Concern. Two major questions about desegregation were raised: (1) Do suburban learning environments provide positive educational experiences for inner-city adolescents?, and (2) What are the coping strategies used by students to persist in these schools? The author shows the effects of desegregation on the students in each of the schools. A major finding is that desegregation effort does not necessarily foster race relations.

Murray, S.R. (1985). *Investigating and understanding the educational needs of Black girls.* American Institutes for Research: Washington, DC. (ERIC Document Reproduction Service No. ED 267166.)

This article discusses three research approaches that focus on Black girls. These approaches suggest: (1) the use of research priorities, (2) the use of personal experiences, and (3) the uses of evaluative studies from existing educational programs, such as the LINCKS program created in Washington, D.C., in 1982.

Scott-Jones, D., and Clark, M. (1986). The school experiences of Black girls: the interaction of gender, race, and socioeconomic status. *Phi Delta Kappan* 67(7), 520-526.

This is a review of the educational experiences of Black girls in schools as influenced by gender, race, and economic status. The investigators report that all three factors significantly impact the psychosocial and intellectual development of Black girls. An analysis of the literature reveals that teachers perceive Black girls as more socially than academically competent, that the educational environment is negatively biased against Black girls, and that attending to sex equity should benefit both Black and White students. The major recommendation is for more research which covers all three variables individually.

Shofield, J.W. and Francis, W.D. (1982). *An observational study of peer interaction in racially-mixed accelerated classrooms.* Bethesda, Md.: National Institute of Health.

This is a study of peer interaction in four racially mixed classrooms with a population of 69 White and 32 Black eighth-grade children. The investigators found more cross-race peer interaction among this population than in previous studies. The students, however, tended to interact more with peers of their own race than with peers of another race. Girls exhibited strong race preference while interactions of boys were more mutual. The study concludes that interactions within-race were more social, and interactions cross-race interactions were more task-oriented.

Sims, R. (1983). Strong Black girls: a ten-year-old responds to fiction about Afro-Americans. *Journal of Research and Development in Education, 16*(3), 21-28.

This is a report of an interview with a young Black female adolescent who enjoyed reading books about Black girls. Reactions and responses to books about Afro-Americans are discussed. The interview contains two parts: (1) research on the response to content of such books and (2) an analysis of approximately 150 books of contemporary realistic fiction about Afro-Americans. Insights into what young adolescent females want in fiction about Afro-Americans are offered.

Smith, E.J. (1982). The Black female adolescent: a review of the education, career and psychological literature. *Psychology of Women Quarterly 6*(3), 261-288.

This is a review of the research on the socialization of Black adolescent females that refutes the notion that Black families encourage females to achieve or aspire to higher educational and career levels than their male counterparts. Black females in high school tend to have higher educational and career aspirations than both Black males and White females. The study suggests that school desegregation adversely affects the educational and career aspirations of Black females more than Black males. Attending predominately White institutions may have a similar negative effect on the self-concept and feelings of acceptance among Black females. Much of the literature suggests that whatever educational and career successes Black adolescent females attain are accomplished despite incredible odds.

Taylor-Gibbs, J. (1985). Psychosocial adjustment of urban Black adolescent females. *SAGE: A Scholarly Journal on Black Women, 2*(2), 28-36.

This study makes a comparison of a multiethnic sample of 387 7th and 9th grade adolescent females enrolled in public schools in the San Francisco Bay area. The ethnic composition of the group was 38 Asians (9.8%), 204 Blacks (52.7%), 23 Hispanics (5.9%), 116 Whites (30%), and 6 American Indians (1.6%). A psycho-ethnographic approach was used to gather data for the study and it included measures on self-esteem, educational and vocational expectations, psychological functioning, and personal interviews. The results showed that Black females were satisfied with themselves and possessed high educational and career aspirations. In comparison with White students, Black students were more similar than different in overall attitudes and aspirations. The author also gives recommendations for promoting healthy Black adolescent females.

Thomas, V.G., and Ahields, L.C. (1987, Spring). Gender influencer on work values of Black adolescents. *Adolescence, 22*(85), 37-43.

This study examined the work values and key influencer on 146 Black male and female urban students. The results showed that both males and females valued intrinsic and extrinsic rewards of work. Females more than males, however, valued specific work values such as "making lots of money" and "doing something for others." The key influencer for both males and females was of the same-race and same-sex, which suggests that Black youth do recognize the significance of role models in the community.

Timberlake, C.H. (1981, October). *Attitudinal differences of Black female secondary students which may influence their graduating from high school.* Paper presented at the meeting of the National Black Child Development Institute, Washington, D.C.

The purpose of this study of secondary Black females is to determine if persisters and non-persisters attitudes were influenced by peers, teachers, school work, and the school environment. The results suggest that a positive attitude toward school work and school in general contribute significantly in aiding Black females to complete high school.

Winters, A.S., and Frankel, J. (1984). Women's work role as perceived by lower status White and Black female adolescents. *Adolescence, 29*(74), 403-415.

This article discusses the results of a study on Black and White female adolescents attending an alternative school on the perceptions of women's work roles. The results indicate no significant differences between the two groups of women. Both groups of women had egalitarian views of women's roles. Two subscales on the questionnaire revealed that they differed greatly in their perceptions of women in the home. In terms of sex-role development, both groups maintained the importance of establishing a sense of worth in relationship to one's work.

Other References

Black Girls and Adolescents

Allen, W. (1978). Race, family setting and adolescent achievement orientation. *Journal of Negro Education, 47*(3), 230-243.

Butler, A. (1987). *Black girls and schooling: A directory of strategies and programs for furthering the academic performance and persistence rate of Black females K-12.* Manhattan: University of Kansas.

Carter, C.J. (1988). Black female students: Issues and considerations for teachers of teachers. *Educational Considerations, 15*(1), 31-36.

Doughty, R.N., and Doughty, J.J. (1985). Toward a meaningful education Black Girls. *SAGE: Scholarly Journal on Black Women. 1*(1), 12-13.

Fleming, J. (1978). Fear of success, achievement-related motives and behavior in Black college women. *Journal of Personality, 46,* 694-716.

Fleming, J. (1984). *Blacks in College.* San Francisco: Jossey-Bass.

Gibbs, J.T. (1985). City girls: Psycho-social adjustment of urban Black adolescent females. *SAGE: Scholarly Journal on Black Women, 2*(2), 28-38.

Guy-Sheftall, B., and Bell-Scott, P. (1989). Finding a way: Black women students in the academy. In C. Pearson, P.G. Touchton, and D.L. Shavlik (Eds.). *Educating the majority: Women challenge tradition in higher education.* New York: Macmillan.

Harrison, A.O. (1974, Spring). Dilemma of growing up Black and female. *Journal of Social and Behavioral Sciences, 20*(2), 28-41.

Zane, N. (1988). *In their own voices: Young women talk about dropping out.* Washington, D.C.: Now Legal Defense and Education Fund.

Career/Occupational Choice

Allen, W. (1979). Family roles, occupational statuses, and achievement orientations among Black women in the United States. *Signs: Journal of Women in Culture and Society, 4*(4), 670-686.

Bell-Scott, P. (1977). Preparing Black women for non-traditional professions: Some considerations for career counselors. *Journal of the National*

Association of Women, Dean, Administrators and Counselors, 40, 136-139.

Burlew, K.A. (1978). Career educational choices of Black females. *Journal of Black Psychology, 3*(2), 89-102.

Corcoran, M. (1980). The employment and wage consequences of teen age women's nonemployability development. In *Research on youth employment and employability development: The youth employment problem; Dimensions, causes and consequences.* (Youth Knowledge Development Report 2.9), Washington, D.C.: U. S. Department of Labor.

Davidson, J.P. (1980). Urban Black youth and career development. *Journal of Non-White Concerns in Personnel and Guidance, 3*(8), 119-140.

Dillard, J. and Perrin, D. (1980). Puerto Rican, Black and Anglo adolescents: Career aspirations, expectations, and maturity. *Vocational Guidance Quarterly, 28,* 313-321.

Gurin, P., and Gaylord, C. (1976). Educational and occupational goals of men and women at Black colleges. *Monthly Labor Review,* 10-16.

Hall, J.G. (1973). An examination of some social psychological determinants of the occupation decision-making of urban high school seniors (Doctoral dissertation, University of Pennsylvania, 1974.) *Dissertation Abstracts International, 34,* 5331A-5332A. (University Microfilms No. 74-2418.)

Hoffman, E.P. (1987). Determinants of youths' educational and occupational goals: Sex and race differences. *Economics of Education Review, 6*(1), 41-48.

Omrvig, C.P., and Darley, L.K. (1972). Expressed and tested vocational interests of Black inner-city youth. *Vocational Guidance Quarterly, 21,* 109-114.

Roderick, R.D. and Davis, J.M. (1973). *Years for decision: A longitudinal study of the educational and labor market experiences of young women.* Volume two. Columbus: Ohio State University.

Smith, E.J. (1976). Reference group perspectives and the vocational maturity of lower socioeconomic Black youth. *Journal of Vocational Behavior, 8,* 321-336.

Smith, E.J. (1981). The career development of young Black females: The forgotten group. *Youth and Society, 12*(3), 277-312.

Sprey, J. (1962). Sex differences in occupational choice patterns among Negro adolescents. *Social Problems, 10,* 11-23.

Stevenson, S. (1975). Counseling Black teenage girls. *Occupational Outlook Quarterly, 19*(2), 1-13

Wallace. P.A. (1974). *Pathways to work.* Lexington, Mass.: Lexington Books.

Wallace, P.A., Datcher, L. and Malveaux, J. (1980). *Black women in the labor force.* Cambridge, Mass.: Massachusetts Institute of Technology.

William T. Grant Foundation Commission on Work, Family and Citizenship (1988). *The forgotten half; Non-college youth in America.* Washington, D.C.: William T. Grant Commission.

Winter, A.S., and Frankel, J. (1984). Women's work role perceived by lower status White and Black female adolescents. *Adolescence, 29*(74), 403-415.

School/Learning Environments

Baron, R., Tom, D., and Cooper, H. (1985). Social class, race and teacher expectations. In J. Dusek and G. Joseph (Eds.), *Teacher Expectancies.* Hillsdale, N.J.: Lawrence Erlbaum, pp. 251-269.

Cooper, H.M. (1979). Some effects of preperformance information on academic expectations. *Journal of Educational Psychology, 71,* 375-380.

Cornbleth, C., and Korth, W. (1980). Teacher perceptions and teacher-student interaction in integrated classrooms. *Journal of Experimental Education, 48,* 259-263.

Crain, R.L., Mahard, R.E., and Narot, R.R. (1982). *Making desegregation work: How schools create social climates.* Cambridge: Ballinger.

Davidson, H., and Lang, G. (1980). Children's perceptions of their teachers' feelings toward them related to self-perception, school achievement and behavior. *Journal of Experimental Education, 29*(2), 331-346.

DeBord, L.W., Griffith, L.J., and Clark, M. (1977). Race and sex influences in the schooling process of rural and small town youth. *Sociology of Education, 42*(2), 85-102.

Dusek, J., and G. Joseph (Eds.) (1985). *Teacher Expectancies.* Hillsdale, N.J.: Lawrence Erlbaum.

Fordham, S., and Ogby, J.U. (1986). Black students' school success: Coping with the "Burden of Acting White." *Urban Review, 13*(3), 176-206.

Hare, B. (1979). *Black girls: A comparative analysis of self-perception and achievement by race, sex, and socioeconomic background.* (Report No.

271.) Baltimore, Md.: Johns Hopkins University, Center for Social Organization of Schools.

Journal of Negro Education. (1987). (Special Issue on the Black Child's Home Environment and Student Achievement), *56*(1).

Lightfoot, S.L. (1978). *Worlds apart: Relationships between families and schools.* New York: Basic Books.

Pollard, D. (1979). Patterns of coping in Black school children. In A.W. Boykin, A.J. Franklin, and F. Yates. (Eds.). *Research directions of Black psychologists.*

Rosenthal, R., and Jacobsen, L. (1968). *Pygmalion in the classroom: Teacher expectations and pupils' intellectual development.* New York: Holt Rineholt and Winston.

Sadker, D., and Sadker, M. (1985). *Sex equity handbook for schools.* New York: Longman Press.

Shakeshaft, C. (1987). A gender at risk. *Phi Delta Kappan, 67*(7), 499-503.

Simons, B. (1980). Sex role expectations of classroom teachers. *Education, 100*(3), 249-259.

Timberlake, C. (1981). Attitudinal differences of Black female secondary students which may influence their graduating from high school. *High School Journal, 66*(2), 123-129.

Washington, V. (1980). Teachers in integrated classrooms: Profiles of attitudes, perceptions, and behavior. *Elementary School Journal, 80*(4), 193-201.

Washington, V. (1982). Racial differences in teacher perceptions of first and fourth grade pupils on selected characteristics. *Journal of Negro Education, 51*(1), 60-72.

Wiley, M.G., and Eskilson, A. (1978). Why did you learn in school today? Teachers' perceptions of causality. *Sociology of Education, 51,* 261-269.

Woolridge, P., and Richman, C. (1985). Teachers' choice of punishment as a function of student's gender, age, and IQ level. *Journal of School Psychology, 23,* 19-29.

Social Interactions in Desegregated Schools

Clark, M.L., and Ayer, M. (1986, April). Friendship expectations and the evaluations of present friendships: Effects of reciprocity, gender and race. Paper presented at the Annual meeting of the American Educational Research Association, San Francisco, Calif.

Damico, S.B. (1985, April). Social interactions in middle schools effects of organizational structure. Paper presented at the Annual Meeting of the American Educational Research Association, Chicago, Ill.

McKenry, P., Everett, J., Ramseur, H., and Carter, C.J. (1989). Research on Black adolescence: A legacy of cultural bias. *Journal of Adolescent Research, 4*(2), 254-264.

Sager, A.H., and Schofield, J.W. (1980, September). Race and gender barriers: Preadolescent peer behavior in academic classrooms. Paper presented at the meeting of the American Psychological Association, Montreal, Canada.

St. John, N.H., and Lewis, R.G. (1975). Race and the social structure of the elementary classroom. *Sociology of Education, 48,* 346-368.

Teahan, J.E. (1974). The effects of sex and predominant socioeconomic class school climate on expectations of success among Black students. *Journal of Negro Education, 43*(2), 345-355.

Teele, J., and Mayo, C. (1969). School racial integration: Tumult and shame. *Journal of Social Issues, 25*(1), 137-156.

Employment

RONALD L. TAYLOR
UNIVERSITY OF CONNECTICUT

Summary

Despite evidence of significant advances in their educational and occupational status, the labor market position and employment problems of Black adolescents grew worse during the past two decades, reaching what some analysts describe as "catastrophic" proportions in the 1980s. As recently as 1954 rates of employment for Black and White youths were identical (52 percent in each case). In the years that followed, however, employment rates for White youth remained relatively constant, whereas the rates for Black youth fell sharply. By 1980, for example, the employment rate for Black teenagers, 16-19, fell to 27 percent, while the rate for Whites in this age category rose to 53 percent (Larson, 1988). The employment crisis is particularly severe in the inner cities where, by some estimates, the joblessness rate among Black youth approaches 60 percent. As Freeman and Holzer (1986) observe in their analysis of the youth unemployment crisis, the much heralded problem of teenage joblessness is largely a crisis among inner city Black youth: "In many respects, the urban unemployment characteristics of Third World countries appears to have taken root among Black youths in the United States" (p. 3).

The causes of high unemployment among Black youth are multiple in nature, as are its consequences for Black communities and the wider society. Various analyses identify the locus of the problem in deteriorating local economies and functional transformations in urban structures, increased job competition between Black youth and older women in the labor force, increases in the minimum wage, discriminatory employer behavior, increased opportunities for criminal activities as alternative sources of employment and income, inadequate education, lack of marketable skills, and low motivation and/or aspirations on the part of Black youth. Although much remains to be learned regarding the interaction and cumulative effects of these factors on Black youth unemployment problems, recent data reported by Freeman and

Holzer (1986), based on a survey of Black males, ages 16-19, in the inner cities of Boston, Chicago, and Philadelphia provide some important insights. The survey, conducted under the auspices of the National Bureau of Economic Research (NBER), included 2,300 Black males (the survey was limited to males because the employment and other problems of Black females are shown to be different) and is the largest sample of such youths currently available in social science research.

The NBER survey analyzed a variety of factors on both the demand and supply side of the labor market and identified some of the primary determinants of Black youth unemployment. On the demand side, the survey adduced strong evidence that the strength of the local economy or labor market was a major determinant of Black youth joblessness, that is, the higher the level of overall demand for labor in the local economy, the higher the rate of Black youth employment. In short, the level of Black youth employment was shown to be highly sensitive to cyclical changes in the economy. Moreover, the rapid increase in recent decades of the number of women in the labor market was shown to have adversely affected the employment opportunities and wages of Black youth, particularly in the service sector, by filling the entry-level jobs that might otherwise go to these youths. In addition, employer discrimination, both actual and perceived, was found to be a factor in the ability of Black youth to gain employment as well as their performance on the job. Black youth who perceived discriminatory behavior by employers were more likely to be absent from and perform poorly on the job, resulting in high discharge rates and high rates of unemployment among these youths.

Among the important determinants of the employment status of Black youth on the supply side of the labor market identified by the NBER survey were: the employment and welfare status of the family, church attendance, career aspirations, illegal income opportunities, level of education, and high reservation wages (i.e., the wage above the market minimum at which a youth would accept a job). Black youth from families on welfare and who lived in public housing projects were shown to have a much worse experience in the job market than Black youth from nonwelfare but otherwise comparable family backgrounds. The employment problems of these youth appeared to be related to the lack of employment and "connections" of adult family members to the job market, and/or the lack of a strong work ethic in such households, rather than a function of their experiences in female-headed households or patterns of welfare benefits. Churchgoing was also found to exert a significant positive influence on Black youth employment through its effects on school attendance and promotion of socially desirable behavior. Although the causal links in this case were difficult to specify, the churchgoing behavior of Black youth was shown to have an independent and different effect on the joblessness rate among these youth than did other family variables. Youths' attitudes toward work and employment aspirations were also found to be important contributors to unemployment. Youths with positive attitudes toward work and strong long-term career aspirations were much more likely to find work than were youth who lacked such attitudes or aspirations. While Black youth were shown to be highly responsive to economic and social incentives that increased their prospects for employment, growing joblessness among these youth increasingly reflected their responsiveness to negative incentives, that is, drugs and other criminal activities, in recent years. Thus poor employment opportunities and the youth's perception of the low probability of arrest and conviction for criminal activities were shown to have contributed to the increased willingness of Black youth to engage in crime as a source of income, with the result that their attachment to, and success in, the legitimate labor market is diminished. Staying in school and high school graduation were also found to have significant positive effects on employment of Black youths, regardless of the quality of the education received in school. Moreover, youth who did better in school had better employment records than those who did less well. Nearly a third of the longer period that Black youth were unemployed was explained by their relatively high reservation wages. Though Black and White youths maintained comparable reservation wages, the failure of the former to adjust their wage expectations in light of more limited employment prospects, was shown to contribute to their joblessness.

These findings from the NBER survey of Black inner city youths are supported by the results from a variety of other recent studies of youth labor market problems. For example, Freeman and Wise (1982) in their summary of the findings from an earlier study of the causes and consequences of youth labor market problems conducted by economists associated with the NBER, provide supporting evidence for many of the results of the inner-city Black youth survey from their analysis of national data on Black and White youths, as does Iden (1980), in his review of the labor force experience of Black youth during the 1970s. Similarly, Cave's (1985) analysis of data from the 1980 Census on employment and other labor force behavior of Black and White youths, identifies the role of location or region, sex, and family income, in addition to several other factors noted by Freeman and Holzer, in accounting for racial differentials in youth labor market experiences.

For a historical perspective on the decline of Black teenage employment Cogan (1982) provides an important analysis of the impact of reductions in the demand for low-skilled agricultural labor on Black youth employment ratios for the period 1950 to 1970. In addition, Mare and Winship (1984) assess the effects of trends in school enrollment and military service on unemployment levels among Black men aged 16 to 29 during the period 1964 to 1981, noting the substantial contribution of these trends to declining Black employment. The growing significance of poverty in accounting for the labor market problems of Black and White youths is assessed by Sum, Harrington, and Goedicke (1987) in their examination of labor force, employment, and unemployment trends for the period 1979 to 1986, and Larson (1988) provides an excellent review of the literature and analysis of employment patterns among Black and White male teenagers from the period 1950 to the present.

The volume by Osterman (1980) considers the causes and consequences of youth unemployment from a variety of perspectives, using data derived from national surveys, interviews with youth and their employers, and conventional economic sources. Likewise, Thomas and Scott (1979) examine the relevance of four theoretical perspectives employed by sociologists and economists for interpreting current trends in the labor market experiences of Black youths and their implications for social policy. And Anderson's (1980) ethnographic study of Black male youths in the city of Philadelphia, provides a first-hand account of the consequences of widespread unemployment among inner-city youths as reflected in the growing sense of alienation, low self-esteem, crime, and other forms of antisocial behavior, as does Glasgow (1980) in his intensive study of young Black men in the Watts area of Los Angeles.

The volume by Mangum and Seninger (1978) includes a useful synthesis of much of the vast literature on unemployment and related issues among inner-city Black youth published during the 1970s, with suggestions for new policy directions, while Wilson (1987) provides a comprehensive analysis of the role of perverse demographic trends, structural transformations in the economy, and dysfunctional life styles in promoting the rise of inner-city social problems, including Black youth unemployment during the 1980s, and offers a far-reaching policy agenda for improving the life chances of the poor. Duster (1987) likewise focuses on the role of structural transformations in the economy in accounting for the relationship between high rates of joblessness among inner-city Black youth and rising crime, concluding with suggestions for effective social intervention.

Annotated References

Anderson, E. (1980). Some observations on black youth employment. In B.E. Anderson and I.V. Sawhill (Eds.), *Youth employment and public policy* (pp. 64-87). Englewood Cliffs: Prentice-Hall.

Anderson focuses on the growing sense of alienation, low self-esteem, crime, and other forms of antisocial behavior manifested by inner-city Black male youths in response to widespread unemployment and poverty in their neighborhood. This essay is based on in-depth interviews with Black male youths from the inner-city of Philadelphia, who responded to questions about their employment experiences, job prospects, family background, educational background, and general life situation. The author discusses the generally negative work experiences of many of these youths, their attitudes toward work and employment opportunities that were available, their involvement in the underground economy (i.e., that network of informal connections and established means by which money is made illegally), and their growing sense of estrangement from mainstream society. Anderson concludes that only meaningful employment opportunities can renew these youths' commitment to mainstream society and prevent their membership in the growing ranks of the Black underclass.

Cave, G. (1985). Youth joblessness and race: Evidence from the 1980 Census. In C.L. Betsey, R.G. Hollister, and M.R. Papgeorgiou (Eds.), *Youth employment and training programs: The YEDPA years* (pp. 367-409). Washington, D.C.: National Academy Press.

This paper was commissioned by the National Research Council as part of its charge from the U.S. Department of Labor to assess existing knowledge regarding the effectiveness of youth employment and training programs established under the Youth employment and Demonstration Projects Act (YEDPA) of 1977. It compares data from the 1980 Census on employment and other labor force behavior reported for Blacks with that reported for White youths in order to determine whether Black youths experienced special problems in the labor market due to their racial membership, and whether correcting such data for location, education, family income and other variables, would eliminate observed racial differentials. Following an overview of the youth unemployment problem and a discussion of the methodological and interpretative problems associated with empirical research in this area, the author presents analyses of the census data with the use of new structural models developed for this purpose. Large and significant racial differences emerged from the data. These racial differences were shown to vary by sex, region, and school enrollment status, and were accounted for in part by the maintenance of higher reservation wages among Black youths and by "discouraged-worker" effects.

Cogan. J. (1982). The decline in black teenage employment: 1950-1979. *American Economic Review, 72,* 621-636.

This paper examines the precipitous decline in the Black teenage employment ratio during the period, 1950-1970. The author contends that such factors as the rapid increase in the Black youth population, the migration of firms from the central cities to the urban fringe and suburbs, and the growth in social welfare programs had negligible effects on the level of Black youth unemployment during this period. Rather, it was the dramatic reduction in the demand for low skilled agricultural labor, particularly in the South, which was the dominant force behind the decline in aggregate Black teenage employment rations. Black teenagers displaced by the mechanization of agriculture were not absorbed into the nonagricultural sector of the economy in significant numbers during the 1970s because of changes in the minimum wage which was expanded in the 1960s to retail trade, construction, and the service industry. The author concludes that while the agricultural explanation applies to the 1950-1970 period, it does not explain the decline in Black teen employment since the 1970s, especially for northern regions of the country, where other factors were at work.

Duster, T. (1987). Crime, youth unemployment, and the Black urban underclass. *Crime and Delinquency, 33,* 300-316.

The author reviews the literature on the relationship between street crime and unemployment among Black and White youths. He discusses how the labor market has been transformed over the past three decades and the ways in which this development has differentially affected Black and White youths, including their participation in crime. He argues that while unemployment does not cause crime in any linear fashion, there is, nonetheless, a strong relationship between labor market experience and crime. Thus individuals who experience unemployments are more likely to have higher rates of criminal involvements than other youths. A key development in the worsening labor market situation of Black youth, Duster argues, is the deep bifurcation of the labor force, characterized by jobs requiring an array of higher-level skills at the top of the service sector, and a large pool of minimum-wage, part-time, casual jobs at the bottom, with few jobs in between. The article concludes with suggestions for effective intervention and social change.

Freeman, R.B., and Holzer, H.J. (Eds.), (1986). *The Black youth employment crisis.* Chicago: University of Chicago Press.

This volume, containing some eleven papers, and reporting the results of a ground breaking survey conducted under the auspices of the National Bureau of Economic Research (NBER) on inner-city Black youths, explores the history, causes, and features of the employment crisis among these youths. The survey, involving 2,300 Black male youths residing in the inner cities of Boston, Chicago, and Philadelphia, produced detailed data on the largest sample of such youths currently available in social science research, and covered a range of topics from their use of leisure time and work activities during the course of a day, their attitudes toward and desire for work, their use of drugs and involvement in illegal activities, their perception of the labor market, and their family situation. No single factor was found to account for the employment problems of Black youths; rather, a combination of factors – on both the demand and supply sides of the labor market – were shown to have contributed to their worsening employment situation. Among the major factors shown to influence the employment prospects of Black youth were: the proportion of women in the labor force; the aspirations and churchgoing behavior of these youths; their willingness to accept low-wage jobs; opportunities for crime; the family's employment and welfare status; the overall state of the local economy; employer discrimination, and the youth's level of education and school performance.

Freeman, R.B., and Wise, D. (Eds.). (1982). *The youth labor market problem: Its nature, causes and consequences.* Chicago: University of Chicago Press.

This volume reports the findings from extensive investigations of the nature, causes and consequences of the youth labor market problem conducted by economists under the auspices of the National Bureau of Economic Research. Among the principal findings presented in the volume are: (1) that youth joblessness is not a wide-spread phenomenon but is concentrated largely among a small group of youths who are disproportionately Black, high school dropouts, and residents of poverty areas; (2) that the major determinants of youth unemployment on the demand side of the economy include the strength of the local labor market, the "industrial mix" in the area where young persons live, and the level of poverty in such areas, the ratio of older to young workers in the local area, and the minimum wage; (3) that the major determinants of youth joblessness on the supply side of the market include the level of education and performance in school, employment status of adult members of the household, and race. Various contributors to the volume note the association of youth unemployment with other widespread social developments, including youth crime, drug use, and suicide.

Glasgow, D.G. (1980). *The Black underclass: Poverty, unemployment and entrapment of ghetto youth.* New York: Vintage Books.

This ethnographic study of a group of Black male youths conducted in Watts, Los Angeles between 1965 and 1968, with a followup in 1975, assesses the effects of poverty, unemployment, and other structural factors on the attitudes and behavior of the fastest growing segment of the nation's underclass. Glasgow presents a detailed analysis of the institutional practices and market dynamics which directly and indirectly contribute to the entrapment of growing numbers of Black youths in the web of poverty, dependency, hopelessness, and despair, and identifies the weaknesses of current intervention strategies in accounting for the failure of social policy to reverse these ominous trends. He documents the role of social service and law enforcement agencies in maintaining and perpetuating the Black underclass, and the failure of community institutions, particularly the schools, to assume their proper responsibility. The volume concludes with suggestions for new approaches to inner-city restoration and new policies designed to reverse the growth of the Black underclass.

Iden, G. (1980). The labor force experience of Black youth: A review. *Monthly Labor Review, 103,* 19-16.

This paper analyzes some of the major factors which affected teenage employment rates by race during the 1970s, including the effects of overall labor market conditions, supply side factors, minimum wage rates, and the impact of youth employment programs established since 1977 to reduce teenage unemployment. Black youths are shown to have been disproportionately affected by the unfavorable job market that characterized much of the 1970s. Moreover, their experience in the labor market during this period was marked by a dual situation: considerable progress in upgrading their occupational and educational status, accompanied by a convergence in Black/White wages, on the one hand, and increasing divergence in the rate of employment, on the other. The author notes that the Black teenage employment-population rate is much less responsive to improving job markets than in previous decades, and suggests the need for a targeted jobs program for low-income Black youth, both in and out of school.

Larson, T.E. (1988). Employment and unemployment of young black males. In J. Gibbs (Ed.), *Young, black, and male in America: An endangered species* (pp. 97-128). Dover, Mass.: Auburn House.

An excellent review of the literature on employment and unemployment problems of Black male youths. The author discusses employment patterns of Black and White male teenagers from the period 1950 to the present, noting major determinants of the structural changes in the economy on the increasing employment problems of these youths. Unlike their White counterparts, Black youth are concentrated in areas of high unemployment, particularly in the trade sector, where the number of entry-level jobs are declining. Larson concludes with a discussion of the policy implications of growing unemployment among Black male youths and recommendations for reversing the trend.

Mangum, G.L., and Seninger, S.F. (1978). *Coming of age in the ghetto: A dilemma of youth unemployment.* Baltimore: Johns Hopkins.

This volume synthesizes much of the vast literature on unemployment among Black inner-city youths published during the decade of the 1970s, including summaries of government data series and special research reports. The authors contend that the major causes of declining employment among ghetto youths are a function of recent and perverse population trends, transformations in local economies, and the spread of dysfunctional life styles in central cities. They examine the nature and magnitude of population increases and shifts in central cities, and their consequences for the labor force participation of Black youths and inner-city social problems. In addition, the influence of family structure and income, youth life styles, and attitudes toward work on the employment experiences of Black youths are assessed. The book concludes with a summary of major findings and their research and policy implications.

Mare, R.D., and Winship, C. (1984). The paradox of lessening racial inequality and joblessness among black youth: Enrollment, enlistment, and employment, 1964-1981. *American Sociological Review, 49,* 39-55.

The authors attempt to reconcile the worsening employment status of Black teenagers and young adults with improvements on other socioeconomic indicators in recent decades. More specifically, they examine the effects of trends in school enrollment and military services on unemployment levels among Black and White men aged 16 to 29 from 1964 to 1981. They argue that increased joblessness among young Black males result in part from changes in the structure and timing of their movement from schooling and military service to work, and hypothesize that: (1) young Blacks, much more than young Whites, are increasingly substituting schooling and military service for work, (2) that this tendency has reduced average years of civilian work experience for young Blacks, and (3) that this higher retention rate of young Blacks in the military and in school has reduced the average attractiveness to employers of the relatively smaller out-of-school civilian youth population that remains. Empirical assessment of these hypotheses, using data from the Current Population Surveys of 1964 through 1981, shows that they account for a substantial part of the disparity in unemployment among Black and White men aged 16 to 29 during this period.

Osterman, P. (1980). *Getting started: The youth labor larket.* Cambridge: MIT Press.

This volume addresses a series of important questions on the nature of the youth labor market: How does the youth labor market work? How do youths find jobs: What are youths' attitudes toward work, how do these attitudes change over time, and how do they affect labor market behavior: Why is youth unemployment rates so high, and why have they seemingly worsened in recent years? Why is unemployment so much higher among Black youths than Whites, and why has the unemployment differential grown in the face of evidence that in other respects the labor market's treatment of Black youths has improved modestly in recent years? Does unemployment have long-term consequences for youth and do such consequences vary with the group? Such questions are analyzed from a variety of perspectives with the use of data drawn from national surveys, interviews with youth and their employers, and conventional economic sources. Chapter 6 of this volume is devoted exclusively to racial differentials in youth unemployment, where several explanations for the deterioration in the labor market situation of Black youths are advanced.

Sum, A.M., Harrington, P.E., and Goedicke, W. (1987). One-fifth of the nation's teenagers: Employment problems of poor youth in America, 1981-1985. *Youth and Society, 18,* 195-237.

This paper provides an overview of labor force, employment, and unemployment developments for youth in the aggregate and for Black and White youth separately during the period 1979 to 1986. Particular attention is given to the decline in the number of full-time job opportunities for youth and the continuing reduction in the nation's goods-producing industries, and the implications of these trends for youth joblessness. Also examined is the labor force behavior and experiences of the growing number of poor youth, and the nature of their labor market problems. While the employment situation of all major subgroups of the poor youth population (high school students, dropouts, high school graduates, males, females, Whites, Blacks, and Hispanics) is shown to have deteriorated since the early 1980s, Black youths from poverty families continue to encounter the most severe employment difficulties of all youth subgroups. The authors conclude that the need for a national policy response to the pervasive and severe joblessness among poor youth in general, and poor Black youth in particular, appears to be greater today than at the start of the decade.

Thomas, G.E., and Scott, W.B. (1979). Black youth and the labor market: The unemployment dilemma. *Youth and Society, 11,* 163-189.

The causes and consequences of Black youth unemployment are examined in this paper from four theoretical perspectives employed by sociologists and economists in their analyses of these phenomena: functional theory of stratification, conflict or Marxist theory, human capital and dual labor market theories. The implications of each of these theoretical perspectives for social policy and intervention are discussed and synthesized by the authors. They contend that most previous efforts aimed at reducing unemployment among Black youths have focused more on eliminating individual-level deficiencies than on reducing imperfections in the labor market or structural inequalities. In their view, increasing the level of access of Black youth to the labor market can be achieved more effectively through a process of "sponsored mobility," that is, through effective social networks and sponsorship groups which function to prepare disadvantage youth for employment and facilitate their entry into the labor market. The advantages and limitations of such an approach are discussed in the context of current policies and practices at the federal and state levels.

Wilson, W.J. (1987). *The truly disadvantaged: The inner city, the underclass, and public policy.* Chicago: University of Chicago Press.

This book of essays addresses a wide range of issues relating to the recent emergence of the Black underclass in the inner-cities across the country, including the rise in Black youth unemployment, out-of-wedlock births, female-headed households, welfare dependency, violent crimes, and other social problems. Wilson offers a comprehensive explanation for the rise of such problems and argues for a broad policy agenda that goes beyond race-specific solutions to strategies which attack the more fundamental problems of economic organization. In this penetrating analysis, Wilson shows how a complex of factors and recent developments have contributed to the growth of inner-city social problems. Central to the rise of the Black underclass and it associated problems has been the transformation of the urban economy, accompanied by increasing rates of poverty and social isolation among economically disadvantaged Black families concentrated in inner cities. Wilson concludes his analysis with a critique of race-specific policies, recommending, instead, universal programs designed to promote full employment, balanced economic growth, and manpower training and education programs which he views as essential to improvements in the life chances of the truly disadvantaged, especially inner-city Black youths.

Other References

Abowd, J.M. and Killingsworth, M.R. (1984). Do minority/white unemployment differences really exist? *Journal of Business and Economic Statistics, 2,* 64-72.

Adams, A.V., and Mangum, G. (1978). *The Lingering Crisis of Youth Unemployment.* Kalamazoo: W.E. Upjohn Institute.

Al-Salam, N., Quester, A., and Welch, F. (1981). Some determinants of the level and racial composition of teenage employment. In S. Rottenberg (Ed.), *The Economics of Legal Minimum Wages.* Washington, D.C.: American Economics Institute.

Anderson, B. (1981). How much did the programs help minorities and youth? In E. Ginzberg (Ed.), *Employing the unemployed.* New York: Basic Books.

Anderson, B. (1986). Youths and the changing job market. *Black Enterprise, 16,* 25.

Anderson, E. (1985). The social context of youth employment programs. In C.L. Betsey, R.G. Hollister, and M.R. Papageorgiou (Eds.), *Youth employment and training programs: The YEDPA years* (pp. 348-366). Washington, D.C.: National Academy Press.

Andrisani, P. (1977). Internal-external attitudes, personal initiative, and the labor market experience of black and white men. *Journal of Human Resources, 12,* 308-338.

Barton, M., Farkas, G., Kushner, K., and McCreary, L. (1985). White, black, and hispanic male youths in central city labor markets. *Social Science Research, 14,* 266-286.

Bassi, L.J., Simms, M.C., Burbridge, L.C., and Betsey, C.L. (1984). *Measuring the effects of CETA on youth and the economically disadvantaged.* Washington, D.C.: Urban Institute.

Becker, B., and Hills, S. (1980). Teenage unemployment: Some evidence of the long-term effects. *Journal of Human Resources, 15,* 354-372.

Betsey, C.L. (1978). Differences in unemployment experience between blacks and whites. *American Economic Review, 68,* 192-197.

Blau, F.D., and Kahn, L.M. (1981). Race and sex differences in quits by young workers. *Industrial and Labor Relations Review, 34,* 563-577.

Borus, M.E. (Ed.). (1980). *Pathways to the future,* vol. 2: *The national longitudinal survey of youth labor market experience in 1980.* Columbus: Ohio State University, Center for Human Resource Research.

Bowman, P.J. (1984). A discouragement-centered approach to studying unemployment among black youth: Hopelessness, attributions, and psychological distress. *International Journal of Mental Health, 13,* 68-91.

Congressional Budget Office. (1982). *Improving youth employment prospects: Issues and options.* Washington, D.C.: Congressional Budget Office.

Cooper, R.V. (1978). *Youth labor markets and the military.* (Rand paper Series.) Santa Monica, Calif.: Rand Corporation.

Davidson, J.P. (1980). Urban black youth and career development. *Journal of Non-White Concerns in Personnel and Guidance, 8,* 119-140.

Endriss, J.R., and Froomkin, J. (1980). *The labor market experiences of 14-21 year olds: Research on youth employment and employability development.* Washington, D.C.: Government Printing Office.

Farkas, G., Smith, D.A., and Stromsdorfer, E.W. (1983). The youth entitlement demonstration: Subsidized employment with a schooling requirement. *Journal of Human Resources, 18*, 557-573.

Freeman, R.B., and Holzer, H.J. (1985). Young blacks and jobs: What we now know. *Public Interest, 78*, 18-31.

Gibbs, J.T. (1984). Black adolescents and youth: An endangered species. *American Journal of Orthopsychiatry, 54*, 6-21.

Ginzberg, E. (1979). *Good jobs, bad jobs, no jobs.* Cambridge, Mass.: Harvard University Press.

Grant, J.H., and Hamermesh, D.S. (1981). Labor market competition among youths, white women and others. *Review of Economics and Statistics, 63*, 354-60.

Hills, S.M. (1986). *The changing labor market: A logitudinal study of young men.* Lexington, Mass.: Lexington Books.

Holzer, H.J. (1986). Reservation wages and their market effects for black and white male youth. *Journal of Human Resources, 21*, 157-177.

Holzer, H.J. (1986). Are unemployed Black youth income maximizers? *Southern Economic Journal, 52*, 777-784.

Holzer, H.J. (1987). Informal job search and Black youth unemployment. *American Economic Review, 77*, 446-452.

Isralowitz, R.E., and Singer, M. (1987). Long-term unemployment and its impact on Black adolescent work values. *Journal of Social Psychology, 127*, 227-229.

Jeffries, J.M. (1986). *Demographic trends and youth employment policy: A look to the year 2000.* New York: New York University, Urban Research Center.

Macleod, J. (1987). *Ain't no makin' it: Leveled aspirations in a low-income neighborhood.* Boulder, Colo.: Westview Press.

Mathematica Policy Research, Inc. (1979). *Young Black men employment study.* Princeton, N.J.: Mathematica Policy Research.

Malveaux, J. (1989). Transitions: The Black adolescent and the labor market. In R. Jones (Ed.), *Black adolescents* (pp. 267-289). Berkeley, Calif.: Cobb and Henry.

Meyer, R., and Wise, D. (1982). The transition from school to work: The experience of Blacks and Whites. *NBER Working Paper, #1007.* Cambridge, Mass.: National Bureau of Economic Research.

Newman, M.M. (1979). The labor market experience of Black youth, 1954-1978. *Monthly Labor Review, 102,* 19-27.

Osterman, P. (1980). The employment problems of Black youth: A review of the evidence and some policy suggestions. In Vice President's Task Force on Youth Employment, *A review of youth employment problems, programs and policies, Vol. II.* Washington, D.C.: U.S. Government Printing Office.

Phillips, L., and Votey, H.L. (1984). Black women, economic disadvantage, and incentives to crime. *American Economic Review, 74,* 293-297.

Pollard, T.K. (1984). Changes over the 1970s in the employment pattern of Black and White young men. In M.E. Borus (Ed.), *Youth and the labor market.* New Brunswick, N.J.: Rutgers University, Institute of Management and Labor Relations.

Price, C.W., and Jarvis, C.H. (1982). An examination of the variables related to minority youth employment. *Journal of Employment Counseling, 19,* 67-75.

Raelin, J.A. (1980). *Building a career; The effect of initial job experiences and related work attitudes on later employment.* Kalamazoo, Mich.: Upjohn Institute for Employment Research.

Ragan, J.F. (1988). Testing for employee discrimination by race and sex. *Journal of Human Resources, 23,* 123-137.

Reubens, B.G., Harrison, J.A., and Rupp, K. (1981). *The youth labor force, 1945-1995: A cross-national analysis.* Totowa, N.J.: Allanheld, Osmun.

Seeborg, I., Seeborg, M., and Zegeye, A. (1986). Training and labor market outcomes of disadvantaged Blacks. *Industrial Relations, 25,* 1.

Shapiro, D. (1984). Wage differentials among Black, Hispanic, and White young men. *Industrial and Labor Relations Review, 37,* 570-581.

Shaw, J.S. (1984). The case for paying teenagers a lower minimum wage. *Business Week, 2836,* 104.

Simms, M.C., and Leitch (1983). *Determinants of youth participation in employment and training programs with a special focus on young women.* Washington, D.C.: Urban Institute.

Spaights, E., and Dixon, H.E. (1986). Black youth unemployment: Issues and problems. *Journal of Black Studies, 16,* 385-396.

Straszheim, M. (1980). Discrimination and the spatial characteristics of the urban labor market for Black workers. *Journal of Urban Economics, 7,* 119-140.

Swinton, D.H., and Morse, L.C. (1983). *The source of minority youth employment problems.* Washington, D.C.: Urban Institute.

Taylor, R.L. (1987). Black youth in crisis. *Humbolt Journal of Social Relations, 4,* 106-132.

United States Commission on Civil Rights. (1982). *Unemployment and underemployment among Blacks, Hispanics, and women.* Washington, D.C.: U.S. Government Printing Office.

Venti, S.F. (1984). The effects of income maintenance on work, schooling, and non-market activities of youth, *Review of Economics and Statistics, 66,* 16-25.

Wallace, P.A. (1974). *Pathways to work-unemployment among Black teenage females.* Lexington, Mass.: Heath Lexington Books.

Westcott, D. (1977). The nation's youth: An employment perspective. *Worklife, 2,* 13-19.

White, C.E. (1981). The peripheralization of Blacks in capitalist America: The crisis of Black youth unemployment and the perpetuation of racism. *Catalyst, 3,* 115-128.

William T. Grant Foundation. (1988). *American youth: A statistical snapshot.* Washington, D.C: Wm. T. Grant Foundation, Commission on Work, Family and Citizenship.

Williams, T., and Kornblum, W. (1985). *Growing up poor.* Lexington, Mass.: Lexington Books.

Williams, W. (1977). *Youth and minority unemployment.* Stanford, Calif.: Hoover Institute.

Family-Adolescent Relationships

PATRICIA BELL-SCOTT
UNIVERSITY OF CONNECTICUT

Summary

The tendency in much family social science research has been to document dysfunction and pathology. Nowhere is this tendency more glaring than in the investigation of Black family-adolescent relationships. Before 1975, most research in this area focused predominantly on the effect of father absence and maternal role ambivalence on Black male youth and adolescents (Bell-Scott, 1976). In fact, the allegedly inadequate gender role socialization of males and the attenuated structure of families have been underlying themes in research and social policy pertaining to Black families for the past 40 years.

Despite two decades of interest in gender role development and recent attention to the problems of adolescent parenthood, systematic studies of Black family-adolescent relationships are sparse (Bell-Scott and McKenry, 1986). No unifying theoretical frameworks have emerged; and concepts are often loosely borrowed from a broad array of perspectives; for example, psychoanalytic and role modeling theories. Consistent with previous trends, recent studies remain focused on behavioral difficulties and social problems, such as gang violence, drug abuse, and school failure. Though evidence of the impact of adolescents' behaviors upon family dynamics and the extended family's significance to the well-being of adolescents has increased, studies which explore these issues remain few in number.

In terms of research design and methodology, longitudinal studies that explore family process and dynamics are extremely rare. Most studies have been based on nonrandom samples or cross-sectional surveys. Questionnaires and interviews requiring self-report are the typical means of data collection. Moreover, urban residents and captive or clinical populations (e.g., adolescents participating in a program for teen parents or the economically disadvantaged) are disproportionately represented in the literature.

Since 1980 more attention has been devoted to the intersection of race, class, and gender as variables in family dynamics as well as in the research process. For example, many researchers now attempt to match interviews and interviewees along racial/ethnic and gender lines. And yet, though ethnocultural and class differences exist within most large, urban communities, researchers continue to ignore these differences or underestimate their significance. Myers (1982) suggests that ethnocultural background (e.g., Haitian versus continental U.S. southern heritage) may be a critical variable in family-adolescent relationships in cities where sizeable Black ethnic enclaves thrive.

Current research on family-adolescent relationships suggests that: (1) The extended family is central to the well-being of most adolescents – especially those who become parents in adolescence (Dressler, 1985; Furstenberg, 1980; Wilson, 1986; (2) The family, particularly the mother, is a critical source of information about many issues (e.g., sexuality, health) for females and often males (Fox and Inazu, 1980; Hendricks, 1980; Joseph, 1984; Stevens, 1984); (3) Adolescent parenthood brings both disadvantages and advantages to the family (Furstenberg, 1980); and (4) Adolescent parenthood impacts dramatically upon the adolescent's family (Poole and Hoffman, 1982).

There is a clear need for more investigation of family-adolescent relationships. Studies which utilize representative samples, examine ethnocultural, gender, and class differences and rely upon multiple methods would be extremely valuable. Also studies which examine the neglected issues of parental role satisfaction, sibling relationships, and family violence are sorely needed.

Leigh and Peterson (1986) suggest several conceptual modifications for future research. These modifications would devote attention to: (1) the influence of adolescents upon other family members (e.g., siblings); (2) the reciprocity between adolescents and parents; (3) the interface between adolescent development and family system; and (4) the impact of events and historical variations on family-adolescent relationships. Finally, though adolescent drug abusers and parents are certainly deserving of continued study, a complete picture of adolescent development requires study of family-adolescent relationships across the spectrum of Black communities and family types.

This section will focus on family-adolescent relationships broadly. Specific attention to adolescent parenthood is addressed in another section.

Annotated References

Allen, W.R. (1985). Race, income and family dynamics: A study of adolescent male socialization processes and outcomes. In M.B. Spencer, G.K.

Brookins, and W.R. Allen (Eds.), *Beginnings: The social and affective development of Black children* (pp. 273-292). Hillsdale, N.J.: Lawrence Erlbaum.

Adolescent males in middle-income, two-parent families were the focus of this study. Data were collected in 1974 in Chicago. The sample consisted of 120 two-parent families, with at least one son aged 14-18 living in the home. Findings suggest racial differences in the dynamics of achievement orientation development. Relative to White mothers, Black mothers occupy more central positions in their families.

Ball, R.E., and Robbins, L. (1985, November). *Parental satisfaction of Black fathers.* Paper presented at the meeting of the National Council on Family Relations, Dallas.

This study reports on the parental role satisfaction of a probability sample of 177 Black fathers from four counties in central Florida and finds that 70 percent perceived their relationships with their children as being "very satisfying." Only seven percent were less than "fairly satisfied." This high level of parental satisfaction persisted regardless of marital status, income or education level, or age of the father. Thus difficulties brought about by factors such as low income and educational levels seem not to impair the parental role satisfaction of these Black fathers. Positively related to satisfaction were social participation—indicated by frequency of contact with relatives, friends, and church. This study provides evidence that in at least the expressive facet of the parental role, family income does not appear to play a major part. The authors conclude that high rates of family break-up and father absence do not necessarily lead to unsatisfactory parent-child relationships, at least in regard to the domain of parental satisfaction investigated.

Bell-Scott, P. (1976). A critical overview of sex roles research on Black families. *Women Studies Abstract,* 5(2), 1-9; Additional reference materials and bibliographies related to sex role development in Black families. *Women Studies Abstracts,* 5(2), 10-14.

This is one of the earliest reviews of the literature on Black sex roles development. Particular attention is devoted to criticism of early research (before 1965), discussion of new research in four areas (i.e., attitudes towards family roles, decision-making and the concept of power in dyadic relationships, role of adult males who do not reside in the family household, and socialization of children into sexual behavior). The need for research in several areas (e.g., sexuality among adolescents, father-daughter relationships) is outlined. Also included is an extensive bibliography.

Bell-Scott, P., and McKenry, P.C. (1977). Some suggestions for teaching about Black adolescence. *Family Coordinator, 26*(1), 46-51.

This paper seeks to explore a neglected area in family life education – Black adolescence. The influence that Black culture has upon the maturation process is discussed. Some suggestions for exploring Black adolescent experiences are outlined for educators and other helping professionals.

Bell-Scott, P., and McKenry, P.C. (1986). Black adolescents and their families. In G.K. Leigh and Peterson, G.W. *Adolescents in families* (pp. 410-432). Cincinnati: South-Western.

This review includes a demographic profile of Black adolescents and their families, a discussion of theoretical perspectives and methodological issues, as well as implications for practice and research. Particular attention is devoted to the issues of identity formation, self-concept, sexuality, and alcohol and drug abuse.

Crastinopol, M.G. (1982). Disturbances in mother-daughter relationships of women offenders. *Counseling and Values, 26,* 172-179.

This is a case study analysis of 12 women offenders (three Black, one Asian, and eight White); most were from low-income families. Crastinopol suggests that the mother-daughter bond has strong repercussions on the daughter's adult sense of self; that deprivations of the old mother-child tie are recreated and revisited in the relationships of women offenders with their own children; and that separation-individuation theory might be a useful perspective in understanding and treating the complex psychosocial problems of women offenders.

Cross, W.E. (1981). Black families and Black identity development: Rediscovering the distinction between self-esteem and reference group orientation. *Journal of Comparative Studies, 12*(1), 19-49.

This is a critical review essay of the research on Black families and Black identity development. Cross argues that when studies of family life and identity development are separated and analyzed, neither offer evidence of negative identity in Blacks; rather it was found that (1) the personal identity of Black children matched that of White cohorts, and (2) Black people have shown a dramatic shift in reference group orientation subsequent to the Black social movement. The author also suggests that racial and personal identity may be unrelated or rather independent domains. This article provides an excellent, analytical review of the themes, perspectives and methodological strategies prevalent in Black family and Black identity research from the 1920s to the late 1960s. This review has particular relevance for research on family-adolescent relationships.

Fox, G.L., and Inazu, J.K. (1980). Mother-daughter communication about sex. *Family Relations, 29,* 347-352; G.L. Fox, and J.K. Inazu, (1980). Patterns and outcomes on mother-daughter communication and sexuality. *Journal of Social Issues, 36,* 7-29.

This study examines patterns of mother-daughter communication on six topics: menstruation, dating and boyfriends, sexual morality, the process of conception, sexual intercourse, and birth control. The sample included 898 mothers and their teenage daughters from Detroit. Fifty-six percent were Black, 44 percent were White. Demographic, attitudinal, and behavioral data were collected in simultaneous face-to-face interviews, each of which lasted about one hour. Interviewers were matched by age and race to the respondents. Approximately half the interviews were conducted at the research site; the remainder were conducted in the respondents home. Most mothers and daughters reported having discussed all six topics. They generally agreed on age at which each topic was introduced and the frequency of communication; but differed in terms of who is seen as the initiator of discussion, how comfortable they are discussing sex, and whether more discussion is wanted. Racial differences were found in communication about sex on the topics of conception, sexual intercourse, and birth control: twenty-five percent of the White mothers compared to 15 percent of Black mothers have never talked about birth control; sixteen percent of Black mothers have never discussed conception compared to 11 percent of White mothers. The investigators concluded that the similarities outweigh the differences across family background characteristics. Mothers who were heads of households were more likely than mothers in male-headed homes to talk frequently with daughters about sex.

Fox, G.L., and Medlin, C. (in press). Accuracy in mothers' perception of daughters' level of sexual involvement: Black and White single mothers and their teenage daughters. *Family Perspectives.*

This study examined the relationships between parental knowledge of teen sexual behavior and quality of parent-teen relationships, patterns of communication about sex, and parental supervision in a sample of mother-daughter dyads from Black and White single-parent homes. Systematic differences were found between accurate and inaccurate mother-daughter dyads in quality of the mother-daughter relationship, communication styles and control behaviors. Few significant race differences were found within accurate and inaccurate groups. However, White mothers were significantly more accurate than Black mothers about daughters' level of sexual involvement. Implications for research and family life educators are suggested.

Furstenberg, F.F. (1980). Burden and benefits: the impact of early childbearing on the family. *Journal of Social Issues, 36*(1), 64-87.

The investigator concluded that unwed pregnancy has some redeeming features for the adolescent's family – such as building family morale, intensifying family exchanges, and filling the empty nest. Moreover, the transition to parenthood is eased by the child care instruction, as well as material assistance, provided by the mother of the teen mother.

Furstenberg, F.F., and Crawford, A.G. (1978). Family support: helping teenage mothers to cope. *Family Planning Perspectives, 10*(6), 322-333.

This study examined the role of family supports in the lives of teen mothers. They found that residential careers of adolescent mothers were closely tied to the family of origin; and that adolescent mothers who remained in the grandmother's household were more likely to complete school and were less likely to continue to receive welfare when compared to girls who set up separate households.

Hogan, D.P., and Kitagawa, E.M. (1985). The impact of social status, family structure, and neighborhood on the fertility of Black adolescents. *American Journal of Sociology, 90*(4), 825-855.

This study, based on a random sample of more than 1,000 Black females in Chicago aged 13-19, reported that the percentage of teens who became pregnant differed substantially by several characteristics: family structure, size, composition; socioeconomic status, neighborhood, and career aspirations.

Joseph, G.I. (1984). Black mothers and daughters: traditional and new populations. *SAGE: A Scholarly Journal on Black Women, 1*(2), 17-21.

This article addresses the lack of research on Black mother-daughter relationships. Issues among heterosexual and lesbian daughter-mother relationships are discussed. The author concludes that conflicting messages about men from mothers, unrealistic expectations among teenage mothers, and homophobia in the Black community are critical issues.

Ladner, J. (1971). *Tomorrow's tomorrow: the Black woman.* New York: Doubleday.

This is a classic study of socialization and maturation of Black girls in an urban setting. Particular attention is devoted to the significance of motherhood in the socialization process. Investigator employed participant-observation technique.

Ladner, J.A., and Gourdine, R.M. (1984). Intergenerational teenage motherhood: Some preliminary findings. *SAGE: A Scholarly Journal on Black Women, 1*(2), 22-24.

This is a report from a pilot study of teenage motherhood. The sample included 30 teenage daughters and their mothers who likewise had their first child during their teenage years. Separate and joint interviews were conducted with these mother-daughter pairs. The majority of the grandmothers were in their thirties; the youngest was 29 years old. The researchers found that grandmothers complained about unmet emotional and social needs, looked to their daughters as a source of emotional support, had many health problems, provided limited contraceptive information to their daughters, and gave their daughters some form of child care but did not assume primary responsibility. Daughters had limited knowledge of effective contraceptive use, negative attitudes about abortion, and difficulty returning to school. The authors conclude that teenage pregnancy among single households reinforces a strong intergenerational pattern of poverty.

LaPoint, B., Picket, M.O, and Harris, B.F. (1985). Enforced family separation: A descriptive analysis of some experiences of children of Black imprisoned mothers. In M.B. Spencer, G.K. Brookins, and W.R. Allen (Eds.), *Beginnings: The social and affective development of Black children* (pp. 239-255). Hillsdale, N.J.: Lawrence Erlbaum.

The sample included 40 Black imprisoned mother-child-caregiver units. The mothers were between 19 and 42; the children were 4 to 12. The caregivers of children were 40 Black extended family members related to the imprisoned mothers. Children were divided into two groups: "young children" between the ages of 4 and 8; "old children" between the ages of 9 and 12. Data revealed strong interdependence in the relationships among incarcerated mothers, children, and caregivers.

Lindblad-Goldberg, M., and Dukes, J.L. (1985). Social support in Black, low-income, single-parent families: normative and dysfunctional patterns. *American Journal of Orthopsychiatry, 55*(1), 42-58.

This study explored structural and functional features of social networks and demographic variables in a sample of 50 clinic-referred and 76 nonclinic Black, low-income, single-parent families. Each family had at least one adolescent living in the home. These authors found that dysfunctional families evidenced asymmetrical reciprocity within network relationships and had more stressful home environments than did nonclinical families.

Peterson, G.W., and Stivers, M.E. (1983). *Significant others for the career plans of low-income Appalachian White and Black youth from the rural*

South. Paper presented at the meeting of the National Council of Family Relations, Minneapolis.

This study investigated the significant others (SOs) who influenced the career decisions of 273 low-income White youth from rural areas of southern Appalachia and 117 Black youth from the rural South, using longitudinal and cross-sectional data. Parents were the most frequent choice of these youth as SOs for career decisions. The greatest diversity of SOs for occupational decisions was chosen during late adolescence. Analyses for race differences in the SO choices failed to support deficit interpretations of the Black family. Implications for interventions to assist low-income Black and White youth from the rural South are discussed.

Poole, C.J., and Hoffman, M. (1981). Mothers of adolescent mothers: How do they cope? *Pediatric Nursing, 7,* 28-31; Poole, C.J., Smith, M.S., and Hoffman, M. (1982). Mothers of adolescent mothers. *Journal of Adolescent Health, 3,* 28-31.

The purpose of this study was to explore the problems faced by forty-four mothers of adolescent mothers and to devise a plan for intervention. Women were interviewed about the impact of grandchildren and daughter's teen pregnancy upon their lives. Seventy-five percent of the women lived in urban areas; 52 percent were Black; and 32 percent had their first child when they were 17 or younger. Three situations were identified: (1) Grandmother is burdened emotionally and otherwise because daughter does not accept responsibility for baby; (2) Grandmother is ashamed of daughter's pregnancy, has little confidence in daughter's judgement, and becomes restrictive in attitudes towards her daughter; (3) Grandmother is available for emotional and financial support – taking care of infant on occasion; however, daughter accepts responsibility for baby. Investigators found that grandmothers in each situation could benefit from educational, financial, social, emotional, and medical support and services (e.g., discussion groups with other mothers of teen mothers); that discussion of problem-solving management techniques would be extremely valuable; that the problems of adolescent pregnancy extend directly to the new grandmothers, and that major problems usually did not occur unless the time and life plans of the grandmother were significantly affected.

Presser, H.B. (1980). Sally's corner: Coping with unmarried motherhood. *Journal of Social Issues, 36*(1), 107-129.

Presser concludes that the survival of the unmarried mother depends heavily upon parental support, particularly from their own mothers, and on public assistance. She also suggests that the role of the unmarried mother's family, especially the well-being of her own mother, must be considered in efforts to assist unmarried mothers and their children.

Reid, P.T. (1982). Socialization of Black female children. In P.W. Berman, and E.R. Ramey (Eds.), *Women: A developmental perspective* (pp. 137-155). Bethesda, Md: National Institutes of Health.

The chapter reviews the literature on sex-role socialization of Black girls with particular emphasis on sex-role development and self-esteem. Race and sex are identified as interacting variables: salient racial differences in children's socialization are also discussed.

Stack, C. (1974). *All our kin: Strategies for survival in a Black community.* New York: Harper and Row.

This is a classic study of Black kinship networks in an urban setting. Investigator employed participant-observation technique. Particular attention is devoted to the significance of maternal and female kinship bonds. The potential impact of researcher's (racial and class) bias in the research process is discussed.

Stevens, J.H. (1988). Social Support, locus of control, and parenting in three low-income groups of mothers: Black teenagers, Black adults, and White adults. *Child-Development, 53*(3), 635-642.

This study examined mother's social support, instrumental use of extended family members and of professionals for help, and sense of personal control, as predictors of parenting skill in 3 groups of low-income women (i.e., 62 Black adult mothers, 62 White adult teens, and 74 Black teen mothers). Black teen and White adult subjects who sought help with child-rearing problems from extended family members were more skillful parents. Black adult parenting mothers' parenting skill was predicted only by locus of control.

Wilson, M.N. (1989). Child development in the context of the Black extended family. *American Psychologist, 44*(2), 380-385.

This article considers child development in the context of the extended family. The author concludes that the current socioeconomic difficulties and unstable interpersonal relations in the Black community have contributed to the persistence of the extended family form; that the effects on children are more indirect than direct; that single mothers who are active participants in an extended-family system have a greater opportunity for self-improvement, work and peer contact than do other mothers; and that the Black elderly donate rather than receive services.

Wilson, M.N. (1986). The Black extended family: An analytical consideration. *Developmental Psychology, 22*(2), 246-258.

This paper provides a critical overview of the literature on the Black extended family. Author examines assumptions, conceptual models and methodological strategies of previous research. A model which explores the life cycle of Black extended families is proposed. Implications for policy, therapy, and research are outlined. Extensive bibliography included.

Wyatt, G.E. (1985). The sexual abuse of Afro-American and White-American women in childhood. *Child Abuse and Neglect, 9,* 507-519.

This study examined the prevalence of child sexual abuse in a multi-stage stratified probability sample of Afro-American and White-American women, 18 to 36 years of age in Los Angeles County. Data were collected by interviewers who matched the subjects' ethnicity. Of the sample of 248 subjects, 154 (62 percent) reported at least one incident of sexual abuse prior to age 18. No statistically significant difference in prevalence rates existed between racial/ethnic groups. The investigator found that young Afro-American pre-teens are most likely to experience contact abuse in their homes, by mostly Black perpetrators, who may be nuclear or extended family members; whereas White women may be at risk during the early childhood and pre-school years by mostly White perpetrators, who may involve them in contact abuse incidents indoors and noncontact abuse incidents out-of-doors.

Other References

Extended Family Relations

Aschenbrenner, J. (1973). Extended families among Black Americans. *Journal of Comparative Family Studies, 4,* 257-268.

Bass, B., et al. (1982). *The Afro-American family: Assessment, treatment and research issues.* New York: Grune.

Bowman, P.J., and Howard, C. (1985). Race-related socialization, motivation, and academic achievement: A study of Black youth in three-generational families. *Journal of American Academy of Child Psychiatry, 24,* 141-143.

Broudin, C.M., et al. (1986). Family interaction in Black, lower-class families with delinquent and non-delinquent adolescent boys. *Journal of Genetic Psychology, 147,* 333-342.

Coates, D.L. (1987). Gender differences in the structure and support characteristics of Black adolescents' social networks. *Sex Roles, 17*(11-12), 667-686.

Coleman, P.P. (1986). Separation and autonomy: Issues of adolescent identity development among the families of Black male status offenders. *American Journal of Social Psychiatry, 6,* 43-49.

Colletta, N.D., and Lee, D. (1983). The impact of support for Black adolescent mothers. *Journal of Family Issues, 4,* 127-143.

Cummings, S. (1977). Family socialization and fatalism among Black adolescents. *Journal of Negro Education, 46,* 62-75.

Daniel, J., Hampton, R.L., and Newberger, E.H. (1983). Child abuse and childhood accidents in Black families: A controlled comparative study. *American Journal of Orthopsychiatry, 53*(4), 645-653.

Dressler, W.W. (1985). Extended family relationships, social support and mental health in a southern Black community. *Journal of Health and Social Behavior, 26,* 39-48.

Edwards, O. (1982). Family formation among Black youth. *Journal of Negro Education, 51,* 111-122.

Fox, G.L. (1986). *Intrafamilial sexual socialization: Patterns and outcomes.* (Final Rep. No. APR000925-01.) Knoxville: University of Tennessee, College of Human Ecology, Department of Child and Family Studies.

Furstenberg, D.D., Nord, C.W., Peterson, J.L., and Zill, N. (1983). The life course of children of divorce: Marital disruption and parental contact. *American Sociological Review, 48*(5), 656-668.

Hare, B. (1982). *The rites of passage: A Black perspective.* (A Youth Development Discussion Paper.) New York: National Urban League.

Hampton, R.L. (1987). *Violence in the Black family: Correlates and consequences.* Lexington, Mass.: Lexington Books.

Hays, W.C., and Mindel, C.H. (1973). Extended kinship relations in Black and White families. *Journal of Marriage and the Family, 25,* 51-57.

Hill, R., and Shakleford, L.(1977). The Black extended family revisited. *Urban League Review, 1,* 18-24.

Hogan, D.R., Petrillo, G.H., and Kitagawa, E.M. (1983). *Family factors in the fertility of Black adolescents.* Chicago: University of Chicago, Population Research Center.

Isaacs, M.R. (1987). *Developing mental health programs for minority youth and their families.* (Technical Assistant Document.) Washington, D.C.: Georgetown University Child Development Center.

Jackson, J.J. (1970). Kinship relations among urban Blacks. *Journal of Social Behaviorial Sciences, 16,* 1-13.

Jackson, J. (1986). Black grandparents: who needs them. In R. Staples (Ed.), *The Black family: Essays and studies.* 3d edition (pp. 186-194). Belmont, Calif.: Wadsworth.

Kellam, S.G. (1979). *Consequences of teenage motherhood for the mother, child and family in a Black urban community.* (Unpublished Progress Report, July 1978-June, 1979.) Washington, DC: National Institute for Child Health Development.

Leigh, G.L., and Peterson, G.W. (1986). *Adolescents in families.* Cincinnati: South-Western.

Lewis, D.K. (1975). The Black family: Socialization and sex roles. *Phylon, 36*(3), 221-237.

McAdoo, H.P. (1980). Black mothers and the extended family support network. In L.F. Rodgers-Rose (Ed.), *The Black Woman* (pp. 125-144). Beverly Hills: Sage.

Martin, E., and Martin, J.M. (1978). *The Black extended family.* Chicago: University of Chicago.

Myers, H. (1982). Research on the Afro-American family: A critical review. In B.A. Bass, G.E. Wyatt, and G.J. Powell, (Eds.) *The Afro-American family: Assessment, treatment, and research* (pp. 35-68). New York: Harcourt Brace Jovanovich.

Peters, M.F. (1975). *Socialization of Black children: A critical review of the literature on parent-child relationships and socialization patterns within the Black family.* (ERIC Document Reproduction Service No. ED 117 225.)

Peters, M., and Massey, G. (1983). Mundane extreme environmental stress in family stress theories: The case of Black families in White America. *Marriage and Family Review, 2,* 193-217.

Reeder, A.L., and Conger, R.D. (1984). Differential mother and father influences on the educational attainment of Black and White women. *Sociological-Quarterly, 25*(2), 239-250.

Scott-Jones, D., and Nelson-Le Gall, S. (1986). Defining Black families: Past and present. In E. Seidman and J. Rappaport (Eds.), *Redefining social problems* (pp. 83-100). New York: Plenum.

Shimkin, D., Shimkin, E., and Frate, D. (1978). *The extended Black family in Black societies.* Chicago: Aldine.

Smith, E.W. (1975). The role of the grandmother in adolescent pregnancy and parenting. *Journal of School Health, 45,* 278-283.

Taylor, R.J. (1986). Receipt of support from family among Black Americans: Demographic and familial differences. *Journal of Marriage and the Family, 48*(1), 67-77.

Thornton, C.I., and Carter, J.H. (1986). Treatment considerations with Black incestuous families. 88th Annual Convention and Scientific Assembly of the National Medical Association (1983, Chicago, Illinois), *Journal of the National Medical Association, 78*(1), 49-53.

Wilson, M.N. (1984). Mothers' and grandmothers' perceptions of parental behavior in three-generational Black families. *Child Development, 55,* 1333-1339.

Wilson, M.N. (1986). Perceived parental activity of mothers, fathers, and grandmothers in three generational Black families. *Journal of Black Psychology, 12*(2), 43-60.

Wilson, M.N., and Tolson, T.F.J. (1983). *An analysis of adult-child interaction patterns in three-generational Black families.* Charlottesville: University of Virginia, Department of Psychology. (ERIC Document Reproduction Service N. ED 256 518.)

Father-Adolescent Relationships

Cazanave, N. (1979). Middle-income Black fathers; An analysis of the provider role. *The Family Coordinator, 28,* 583-593.

Cooke, G. (1974). Socialization and the Black male: Research implications. In L. Gary (Ed.) *Social research and the Black community: Selected issues and priorities* (pp. 76-87). Washington, D.C.: Howard University.

Dennis, R.E. (1980). Homicide among Black males: Social costs to families and communities. *Public Health Reports, 95*(6), 556.

Eberhardt, C., and Schill, T. (1984). Differences in sexual attitudes and likeliness of sexual behaviors of Black lower socioeconomic father-present versus father-absent female adolescents. *Adolescence, 19,* 99-105.

Franklin, C.W., and Pillow, W. (1982). The Black male's acceptance of the prince charming ideal. *Black Caucus Journal, 13,* 3-7.

Gary, L. (Ed.) (1981). *Black Men.* Beverly Hills: Sage.

Hendricks, L.E. (1980). Unwed adolescent fathers: Problems they face and their sources of social support. *Adolescence, 15,* 861-869.

Hendricks, L.E., and Montgomery, T. (1983). A limited population of unmarried adolescent fathers: A preliminary report of their views of fatherhood and the relationship with mothers of their children. *Adolescence, 18,* 201-210.

Jackson, J.J. (1974). Ordinary Black husband-fathers: The truly hidden men. *Journal of Social and Behaviorial Sciences, 20,* 17-19.

McAdoo, J.L. (1981). Involvement of fathers in the socialization of Black children. In H.P. McAdoo (Ed.), *Black families* (pp. 225-237). Beverly Hills: Sage.

Nolle, D.B. (1972). Changes in Black sons and daughters: A panel analysis of Black adolescents' orientations toward their fathers. *Journal of Marriage and the Family, 34*(3), 443-447.

Staples, R. (1982). *Black masculinity.* San Francisco: The Black Scholar.

Mother-Adolescent Relationships

Avery, B.Y. (1985) Breaking the silence about menstruation: Thoughts from a mother/health activist. *SAGE: A Scholarly Journal on Black Women, 1*(2), 30.

Brook, J., et al. (1979). Maternal and adolescent expectations and aspirations as related to sex, ethnicity and socio-economic status. *Journal of Genetic Psychology, 135,* 209-216.

Brookins, G.K. (1985). Black children's sex-role ideologies and occupational choices in families of employed mothers. In M.B. Spencer, G.K. Brookins, and W.R. Allen (Eds.), *Beginnings: The social and affective development of Black children* (pp. 257-271). Hillsdale, N.J: Lawrence Erlbaum.

Bryan-Logan, B.N., and Dancy, B.L. (1975). Unwed pregnant adolescents: Their mother's dilemma. *Nursing Clinics of North America, 9*(1), 57-68.

Collins, P.H. (1987). The meaning of motherhood in Black culture and Black mother-daughter relationships. *SAGE: A Scholarly Journal on Black Women, 4*(2), 3-10.

Dougherty, S.H. (1977). *Becoming a woman in rural Black culture.* New York: Holt, Rinehart and Winston.

Gold, M., and Yanof, D. (1985). Mothers, daughters and girlfriends. *Journal of Personality and Social Psychology, 49*(3), 654-659.

Fischman, S.H. (1977). Delivery or abortion in inner-city adolescents. *American Journal of Orthopsychiatry, 47,* 127.

Fox, G.L., and Inazu, J. (1982). The influence of mother's marital history on the mother-daughter relationship in Black and White households. *Journal of Marriage and the Family, 44,* 143-154.

Furstenberg, F.F. (1976). *Unplanned parenthood: The social consequences of teenage childbearing.* New York: Free Press.

Guy-Sheftall, B. (1982). Mothers and daughters: A Black perspective. *Spelman Messenger, 98,* 4-5.

Horton, C.P., Gray, B.B., and Roberts, S.O. (1976) Attitudes of Black teenagers and their mothers toward selected contemporary issues. *Journal of Afro-American Issues, 4*(2), 172-92.

Inazu, J.K., and Fox, G.L. (1980). Maternal influence on the sexual behavior of teenage daughter: Direct and indirect sources. *Journal of Family Issues, 1,* 81-102.

Jessor, S.L., and Jessor, R. (1975). Transition from virginity to nonvirginity among youth: A social-psychological study over time. *Developmental Psychology, 11,* 473-484.

Joseph, G., and Lewis, J. (1981). *Common differences: Conflicts in Black and white feminist perspectives.* New York: Doubleday.

Kandel, D.B. (1971). Race, maternal authority and adolescent aspiration. *American Journal of Sociology, 76*(6), 999-1020.

Powell, G. (1979). Growing up Black and female. In C. Kopp (Ed.), *Becoming female: perspectives on development.* (pp. 29-66). New York: Plenum.

SAGE: A Scholarly Journal on Black Women. (1985). (Special Issue on Mothers and Daughters), *1*(2).

SAGE: A Scholarly Journal on Black Women. (1987). (Special Issue on Mothers and Daughters), *5*(2).

Wilkinson, D.K. (1984). Black women and their families. *Marriage and Family Review, 7,* 125-142.

Sexuality and Contraception

JOSEPH H. PLECK
WHEATON COLLEGE

Summary

This section primarily covers empirical studies and review articles concerning sexual and contraceptive behavior. Also included is research comparing the background characteristics of adolescent parents and nonparents, and on factors associated with repeat pregnancy. Studies of family interaction in teen families and interaction between teen parents and their own parents or social agencies appear in the chapter on teen parenting. Studies included here either report data for Black adolescents separately within larger samples, analyze race as an explanatory variable within a sample, or use predominantly Black samples.

Current concern about teen pregnancy as a social problem has stimulated great research interest in adolescent sexual and contraceptive behavior. Data from the surveys of national representative samples of adolescents conducted by Zelnik and Kantner in 1971, 1976, and 1979 (females in all years, males only in 1979) indicate that Black adolescents have higher rates of sexual activity and premarital pregnancy than do White adolescents (Zelnik and Kanter, 1980; Zelnik and Shah, 1983). Interestingly, the racial differential in rates of sexual activity is greater for females than for males. At the same time, Blacks compare more favorably to Whites on several other indicators. For example, fewer Black than White females have many sexual partners, and fewer Black females have intercourse very frequently (Zelnik and Kantner, 1977). In addition, rates of teen pregnancy rose less for Blacks than Whites during 1971-1979 (Zelnik and Shah, 1983). Further, rates of later premarital pregnancy subsequent to a first premarital pregnancy are falling for Blacks while rising for Whites (Koenig and Zelnik, 1982). It is also noteworthy that in contrast to the findings from national representative samples, several studies using mixed-race inner-city male samples find little variation in sexual behavior by race or ethnicity (Finkel

125

and Finkel; 1975; Norman, 1977). This may suggest that when social class is controlled, race accounts for relatively little variation in adolescent sexuality.

As reported by females, rates of contraceptive use are somewhat lower among Blacks than Whites, but the rate of utilization of prescription methods (which are more effective than nonprescription methods) is higher for Blacks (Zelnik and Shah, 1983). Nathanson and Becker's (1986) data suggests that somewhat different dynamics are involved for White and Black females in seeking contraceptives from a family planning clinic. While White females reported greater encouragement to seek contraception from the boyfriend and female peers, Black females reported greater support for the clinic visit from their mothers.

Another study illustrating differential correlates of sexual and/or contraceptive behavior is Furstenberg, Moore, and Peterson's (1985) analysis of the 1981 National Survey of Children. Exposure to sex education predicted low rather than high sexual activity among all race-sex groups except Black male adolescents (aged 12-17), among whom low exposure was associated with higher rates of sexual activity.

Other studies investigate correlates of Black teen parenthood. Rivara, Sweeney, and Henderson (1985), for example, found that teen fathers did not differ from nonfathers in age at initiation or frequency of sexual activity, or knowledge of contraception, but that teen fathers less often saw pregnancy as disruptive to educational or vocational plans, and more often had mothers who were teen parents.

In overview, a variety of lines of research within the area of adolescent sexuality and contraception have been established. Many studies in this research literature include Black subsamples or focus predominantly on Blacks. It has become routine for researchers to analyze and report racial similarities and differences in sexual and contraceptive behavior. More work is needed, however, in investigations of possible differential dynamics of sexual (e.g., homosexual behavior) and contraceptive behavior among different racial and ethnic groups.

Annotated References

Belcastro, P.A. (1985). Sexual behavior differences between Black and White adolescents. *Journal of Sex Research*, 21, 55-67.

Using a convenience sample of 98 Black males and females, and 467 White males and females, enrolled in health education courses at a large midwestern university, the two racial groups were more similar than dissimilar in their sexual behavior patterns. The differences that did emerge were: Black males had more interracial coital experience than White males, and White males had more masturbatory experience than Black males. Black females, when compared with White females, were less likely to have performed fellatio, used coitus interruptus, or masturbated a partner.

Center for Population Research, National Institute of Child Health and Human Development. (1986). *Adolescent pregnancy and childbearing–Rates, trends, and research findings from the CPR, NICHD.* Bethesda, Md.: Center for Population Research.

    This report summarizes current national statistics on adolescent pregnancy and childbearing, as well as major recent studies sponsored by CPR, NICHD. During the period 1960-1983, the total number of births to women under 20 declined, while the number of out-of-wedlock births increased, due to declining rates of marriage as resolution to unmarried pregnancy.

Clark, S.D., Zabin, L., and Hardy, D.J. (1984). Sex, contraception, and parenthood: Experiences and attitudes among urban Black young men. *Family Planning Perspectives, 16,* 77-82.

    Eighty-seven percent of 660 Black adolescent males attending an inner-city junior high school and senior high school in Baltimore report that they have had sexual intercourse. Eighty percent of the sexually experienced teenagers have used a contraceptive method, and 60 percent used one at last intercourse. Contraceptive practice is characterized by heavy reliance on male methods: of those using a method at last intercourse, 41 percent relied on the condom; 15 percent withdrawal; and 14 percent on a combination of male and female methods. Use of female methods alone (mostly the pill) accounted for 28 percent of contraceptive practice at last intercourse. Although nearly nine in 10 respondents recognize that boys share a responsibility for preventing pregnancy when they have sex, more than half are willing to tolerate unprotected coitus. Most wish to delay parenthood until their early 20s, but many appear to hold attitudes conducive to out-of-wedlock conception. The mean age they report as "best" for a man to begin intercourse is six years younger than the mean best age to become a parent, which is in turn two years younger than the age they regard as best to get married. Among the high school students, a majority realize that being a father while still in school involves problems for themselves as well as for the girl and baby. Nevertheless, while 34 percent say that they would be "very upset" if they got a girl pregnant in the next six months, 13 percent would not be upset and 12 percent would be happy. Awareness of and accuracy of knowledge about contraceptive methods was also analyzed.

Cutright, P., and Smith, H.L. (1986). Intermediate determinants of racial differences in 1980 U.S. nonmarital fertility rates. *Family Planning Perspectives, 20,* 119-123.

There are four major determinants of racial differences in nonmarital fertility rates in the U.S.: differential sexual activity (exposure to risk), differential in spontaneous and induced abortion, differential contraceptive use (including method efficacy), and differential legitimation through marriage of births conceived out of wedlock. Racial differences in all four indicators encourage higher Black than White nonmarital fertility rates in every age group examined; however, the relative contribution of each determinant to differences in nonmarital fertility varies according to age.

DiClemente, R.J., Boyer, C.B., and Morales, E.S. (1988). Minorities and AIDS: Knowledge, attitudes, and misconceptions among Black and Latino adolescents. *American Journal of Public Health, 78,* 55-57.

The study tested differences in knowledge, attitudes, and misconceptions about AIDS among Black, Latino, and White high school students in San Francisco. White adolescents were more knowledgeable than Black adolescents, and Black adolescents were more knowledgeable than their Latino peers. Less knowledge and prevalent misconceptions about casual contagion of AIDS were associated with greater levels of perceived risk of contracting AIDS, especially among Black and Latino adolescents.

Flick, L.H. (1986). Paths to adolescent parenthood: Implications for prevention. *Public Health Reports, 101,* 132-137.

Flick reviews 79 studies providing information on the correlates of sexual activity, contraceptive use, delivering the child (versus abortion), and keeping the child (versus adoption). Studies including Black adolescents are identified.

Finkel, M.S., and Finkel, D.J. (1975). Sexual and contraceptive knowledge, attitudes and behavior of male adolescents. *Family Planning Perspectives, 7,* 256-260.

The sample consisted of 421 male students enrolled in three northeastern urban high schools. The proportions of Black, White, and Hispanic males in the sample who had experienced coitus, and the proportions using contraception at last intercourse, varied little by ethnicity.

Freeman, E.W., Rickels, K., Huggins, G.R., and Garcia, C. (1984). Urban Black adolescents who obtain contraceptive services before or after their first pregnancy. *Journal of Adolescent Health Care, 5,* 183-190.

This study compares three groups of urban Black teenage females at their enrollment in a contraceptive program and at one-year follow-up. The groups comprise 263 never-pregnant, postabortion, and postpartum teens under age 18 at the initial family planning visit. Self-report questionnaires examined attitudes and information about pregnancy and contraceptive use, sources of contraceptive information, sexual and contraceptive experience, and demographic background factors. Emotional, personality, and psychological factors were assessed with standard measures. Age, partner relationships, and items relating to the mother's communication about contraception and pregnancy were significant variables in the outcome of never-pregnant and delivery of pregnancy. Self-esteem was highest in the never-pregnant group. Personality factors, emotional distress, and social adjustment scores were in the normal ranges and did not differentiate between the groups. Contraceptive uses at follow-up was most consistent in the never-pregnant group.

Freeman, E.W., Rickels, K., Mudd, E.B.H, and Huggins, G.R. (1982). Never-pregnant adolescents and family planning programs: Contraception, continuation, and pregnancy risk. *American Journal of Public Health, 72,* 815-822.

Four hundred urban Black teenage females enrolling in a family planning program before pregnancy were followed for one year to assess factors influencing continuation of contraceptive use. Over half of the follow-up respondents claimed to always use contraception, but nearly half had no sex activity when contacted at follow-up. Sex frequency reported in the sample was low. Background factors of age, grade, and household were associated with contraceptive use and with pregnancy. Girls who had pregnancies were significantly more likely to live in a single-parent household, to have sex more frequently, and to have stated at enrollment that they wanted their first child before age 20. A majority of the sample, nearly all of whom obtained oral contraception, did not know at the one year follow-up any alternative methods for preventing conception, hence many would again be at risk of pregnancy when sex activity resumed.

Furstenberg, F.F., Jr., Morgan, S.P., Moore, K.S., and Peterson, J.L. (1987). Race differences in the timing of adolescent intercourse. *American Sociological Review, 52,* 511-518.

In a national sample of youth aged 15-16, Blacks are roughly four times more likely than whites to report ever having intercourse. This study considers (1) a demographic composition explanation that stresses differential socioeconomic position; (2) an explanation that focuses on the consequences of low socioeconomic position, a higher incidence of female-headed households, or differences in school performance or educational aspirations; and (3) a contextual explanation based on differences in subgroup attitudes and norms. Results provide limited support for the demographic composition argument and stronger support for a contextual subgroup argument. Blacks in predominantly Black classrooms are much more likely to report ever having intercourse. The study further identifies some attitudinal differences between Whites, Blacks, and Blacks in racially homogeneous school settings that could characterize different normative contexts.

Furstenberg, F.F., Moore, K.A., and Peterson, J.A. (1985). Sex education and sexual experience among adolescents. *American Journal of Public Health,* *75,* 1331-1332.

Data from the 1981 National Survey of Children show that 15- and 16-year-olds who have been exposed to sex education are less likely to be sexually experienced, and are neither more nor less likely to discuss sex with parents at home. The negative association between sex education and sexual activity held up for all subgroups except Black males. Black males and females were less likely to have received sex education than White adolescents.

Hayes, C.D. (Ed.) (1987). *Risking the future: Adolescent sexuality, pregnancy, and childbearing,* Vol. 1. Washington: National Academy Press.

This is the summary report of the Panel on Adolescent Pregnancy and Childbearing, National Academy of Sciences. It provides the most comprehensive available current review of trends in adolescent sexuality and fertility, determinants of adolescent sexual behavior and decision-making, consequences of adolescent childbearing, preventive interventions, interventions for pregnant and parenting adolescents, and priorities for data collection, research, policies, and programs. For the working papers providing the basis of this review, see Hofferth and Hayes (1987).

Hardy, J.B., and Duggan, A.K. (1988). Teenage fathers and the fathers of infants of urban, teenage mothers. *American Journal of Public Health, 78,* 919-922.

Data from birth certificates for births in Baltimore in 1983 were used to describe fathers whose child was born to a teenage mother. Four groups were identified: both father and mother were teenagers (12 percent), only the mother was a teenager (14 percent), only the father was a teenager (2 percent), and both parents were aged 20 years or above (72 percent). Within the teenage parent groups, White fathers had lower educational attainment than Black. One in four White fathers was married versus less than 5 percent of Black fathers.

Hendricks, L.E., Robinson-Brown, D., and Gary, L.E. (1984). Religiosity and unmarried Black adolescent fatherhood. *Adolescence, 19,* 417-424.

The relationship between religiosity and unmarried adolescent fatherhood was examined in 48 unmarried Black adolescent fathers and a matched sample of 50 Black adolescent nonfathers in Columbus, Ohio. The results indicated that the fathers did not differ so much from nonfathers in the degree that they are religiously oriented, but in the manner that they give expression to their religious involvement. Fathers were more likely than nonfathers to be responsive to nongroup modes of institutionalized religion (i.e., media forms); whereas the nonfathers' religious involvement was likely to be within institutionalized groups.

Hofferth, S.L., and Hayes, C.D. (Eds.) (1987). *Risking the future: Adolescent sexuality, pregnancy, and childbearing,* Vol. 2: Working Papers and Statistical Appendices.

This is the set of working papers providing the basis for the report of the Panel on Adolescent Pregnancy and Childbearing, National Academy of Sciences (see Hayes, 1987). The individual chapters provide the most comprehensive available current reviews of factors affecting the initiation of sexual intercourse, adolescent sexual behavior as it relates to other transition behaviors in youth, contraceptive decision-making, teen pregnancy and its resolution, health and medical consequences of adolescent sexuality and pregnancy, social and economic consequences of teen childbearing, teen fatherhood, the children of teen childbearers, the effects of programs and policies on adolescent pregnancy and childbearing, the public costs of teenage childbearing, and trends in adolescent sexual and fertility behavior.

Hogan, D.P., and Kitagawa, E.M. (1985). The impact of social status, family structure, and neighborhood on the fertility of Black adolescents. *American Journal of Sociology, 90,* 825-855.

Using data from 1,078 Black females aged 13-19 who lived in Chicago in 1979, this analysis assesses the effects of social class, parent's marital status, number of siblings, neighborhood quality, parental control of dating, having a sister who is a teenage mother, career aspirations, and contraceptive use at first intercourse on fertility. This analysis seeks to improve on previous demographic research by measuring the total effects of these variables on fertility and decomposing them into components due to effects on rates of initial sexual intercourse and the probability of conception among the sexually active. A nonbiasing, continuous-time semi-Markov model is used to identify the net effects of these factors on rates of initial sexual intercourse and pregnancy.

Hogan, D.P., Astone, N.M., and Kitagawa, E.M. (1985). Social and environmental factors influencing contraceptive use among Black adolescents. *Family Planning Perspectives, 17,* 165-169.

Using data from 348 sexually active unmarried Black females and 124 sexually active unmarried Black males aged 13-19 in Chicago, it was found that 28 percent of the young women and 18 percent of the young men used a contraceptive at first intercourse. Statistically significant differences in contraceptive use were found for three social and environmental characteristics: social class, parents' marital status, and neighborhood quality. Among males, social class was the only significant predictor. For both sexes, career aspirations were of marginal significance in predicting contraception. Number of siblings, parental supervision of dating, and having a sister who had become a teenage mother showed no association with contraceptive use. Twenty-five percent of the teenage women who did not practice contraception the first time they had intercourse did so the second time, and 47 percent of those who did not use contraception the second time did so at most recent intercourse. Sixty-three percent of the women used a method at most recent intercourse. Social and environmental variables were found to affect contraceptive use at first intercourse only, and not subsequent initiation of contraception.

Houston, L.N. (1977). Romanticism and eroticism among Black and White college students. *Adolescence, 16,* 263-272.

Questionnaires were administered to students at the four New Brunswick campuses of Rutgers University. The total sample of 1,142 included 89 Black males and 38 Black females. Males were more erotic than females, females were more romantic than males, and the discrepancies were greater for Blacks than for Whites. Although Black males were more erotic than White males, there were few differences between Black and White females.

Koenig, M.A., and Zelnik, M. (1982). Repeat pregnancies among metropolitan-area teenagers: 1971-1979. *Family Planning Perspectives, 14,* 341-344.

A declining proportion of young women who become premaritally pregnant marry during their first pregnancy: 33 percent of metropolitan-area women aged 15-19 in 1971 did so, compared to 16 percent of those interviewed in 1979. Of those surveyed in 1979, almost 50 percent conceived again within 24 months, including 30 percent among those who remained unmarried. Most age, race, and pregnancy outcome groups show a decline in repeat pregnancies, with the exception of White teenagers.

Leigh, G.K., Weddle, K.D., and Loewen, I.R. (1988). Analysis of the timing of transition to sexual intercourse for Black adolescent females. *Journal of Adolescent Research, 3*(3-4), 333-345.

Using the subsample of Black females between 15-19 years of age from the National Survey of Family Growth Cycle III survey (1982), a life course perspective was used to identify the relationship between significant life events and other influences on the timing of the transition to first intercourse. Life events such as dating, as well as other demographic factors such as mother's education and family income, were important influences.

Marsigilio, W. (1987). Adolescent fathers in the United States: Their initial living arrangements, marital experience, and educational outcomes. *Family Planning Perspectives, 19,* 240-251.

Data from a nationally representative longitudinal survey show that 7 percent of young males aged 20-27 in 1984 had fathered a child while they were teenagers, more than three-quarters of them nonmaritally. Overall, young Black men were more likely to have been responsible for a nonmarital first birth than were males of other racial backgrounds, and only 15 percent of Black teenagers lived with their first child shortly after the child's birth, compared with 48 percent of Hispanics, 77 percent of disadvantaged Whites, and 77 percent of nondisadvantaged Whites. While several background variables predicted living with the child at least initially after the birth for White teenage fathers, no variables in the model were significant for Black teen fathers. For nonmarital births occurring before the father graduated from high school, multivariate analysis revealed that living with the child after birth was not related to completion of high school, while being Black was positively associated. The racial difference may mean that norms or social and familial supports are more influential for young Black males in minimizing the possible deleterious effects of teenage fatherhood on schooling.

Marsiglio, W. (in press). Adolescent males' pregnancy resolution preferences and family formation intentions: Does family background make a difference for Blacks and Whites? *Journal of Adolescent Research, 4.*

This study examines high school Black males' preferences, beliefs, attitudes, subjective norms, and intentions concerning pregnancy resolution and family formation decisions. Survey data from a sample of 107 high school males in a midwestern city are used to test Ajzen and Fishbein's social psychological model. Respondents were asked to provide responses to a vignette in which they were responsible for an unplanned pregnancy within the context of a serious relationship. Forty-four percent of the respondents indicated that they would be at least "quite likely" to live with their child and partner, while 11 percent indicated that abortion was their first preference. Respondent's attitudes were much more strongly related to their intentions than were their views of what others would want them to do. The model was particularly powerful for young Blacks whose fathers had a college education. These data are consistent with the notion that a sizeable percentage of adolescent Black fathers involved in serious relationships may be inhibited from realizing their family formation preferences due to social structural barriers.

Moore, K.A., Simms, M., and Betsy, C. (1986). *Choice and circumstance: Racial differences in adolescent sexuality and fertility.* New Brunswick, N.J.: Trans-Action.

The authors review available research concerning information, services, and aspirations regarding education, occupation, and family as factors accounting for racial differences in adolescent sexuality and fertility. Adolescents who are young, Black, male, and have parents with low education have the least knowledge about sexuality and contraception. About half of both Black and White teens receive medical family planning services. Greater emphasis should be placed on getting teens who are sexually active to use available services. Among teens, the abortion rate among Blacks is twice as high as among Whites. The possibility that Whites have higher educational aspirations than Blacks, and that such a difference accounts for Black teens' higher pregnancy rates, was explored and discounted. However, Blacks are more likely to drop out, and dropouts are more likely to become pregnant than teens who remain in school. It does not seem necessary to encourage Black youth to raise their educational aspirations, but efforts are needed to help them achieve their already high aspirations. There is weak evidence that occupational aspirations delay childbearing, and that participation in job training programs reduces fertility. Black teenagers perceive greater tolerance for out-of-wedlock childbearing in their neighborhood than white youth, and are more accepting of premarital sexual activity. Youth from single-parent families appear to be more likely to be sexually active and to become pregnant, and since a majority of Black youth are not raised by two parents, Black youth appear relatively disadvantaged in this regard.

Morrison, D.M. (1985). Adolescent contraceptive behavior: A review. *Psychological Bulletin, 98,* 539-568.

This is a comprehensive review article summarizing the psychologically oriented research literature on adolescent contraceptive use. Descriptive studies, individual difference studies, and theory-based studies from family planning, medical and applied journals are covered, as well as studies in psychology journals. The research suggests that adolescents are largely uninformed about many methods of contraception. They have negative attitudes toward contraception generally and toward using contraceptives. The widespread nonuse of contraception by sexually active adolescents is not irrational, given their levels of information and their beliefs and attitudes. Psychological models using cognitive, emotional, and developmental factors have been used to predict and explain these behaviors, and they hold promise for future research. One section of the review concerns racial and ethnic comparisons.

Nathanson, C.A., and Becker, M.H. (1986). Family and peer influence on obtaining a method of contraception. *Journal of Marriage and the Family, 48,* 513-525.

This study examines the influence of parents, peers, and partners on teenage women's contraceptive-seeking behavior. Data are from a survey of 2,884 unmarried women who were making their first visit to a family planning clinic. The majority of these young women report active participation in, and support for, the clinic visit by significant others. Black female adolescents were found to differ from White female adolescents in reporting relatively higher involvement in the clinic visit by the mother, and lower involvement by the boyfriend or female peers.

Norman, A.J. (1977). Family planning with third-world males. *Health and Social Work, 2,* 139-157.

This is a description of the Young Male Project of the Los Angeles Regional Family Planning Council. As part of the project, data are reported from a sample of 275 Black, Chicano, Asian-American, and American Indian males concerning sexual activity, awareness of birth control methods, and use of the condom.

Pleck, J.H. (in press). Correlates of Black adolescent males' condom use. *Journal of Adolescent Research, 4.*

Using the subsample of sexually active males aged 17-21 in the 1979 National Survey of Young Men, analyses report contraceptive methods used at first and most recent intercourse by 265 Black and 354 non-Black adolescents. Black adolescents reported a somewhat lower rate of condom use at first intercourse (13.2 percent) than did non-Black males (21.8 percent). At most recent intercourse, Black males reported a higher rate of condom use (20.0 percent) than did non-Black males (16.9 percent). The race difference in condom use at first intercourse was evident only among those becoming sexually active at age thirteen or younger.

Polit, D.F., and Kahn, J.F. (1986). Early subsequent pregnancy among economically disadvantaged teenage mothers. *American Journal of Public Health, 76,* 167-171.

This study investigated the antecedents and short-term consequences of an early subsequent pregnancy in a sample of economically disadvantaged teenage mothers. Data were gathered over a two-year period from 675 young mothers living in eight United States cities. Within two years of the initial interview, when half the sample was still pregnant with the index pregnancy, nearly half the sample experienced a second- or higher-order pregnancy. Characteristics of the young women at entry into the study were relatively poor predictors of which teenagers would conceive again by the final interview. An early repeat pregnancy was associated with a number of negative short-term consequences in the areas of education, employment, and welfare dependency, even after background characteristics were statistically controlled.

Rivara, F., Sweeney, P., and Henderson, B. (1985). A study of low socioeconomic status Black teenage fathers and their nonfather peers. *Pediatrics, 75,* 648-656.

Demographic variables, background variables, attitudes, knowledge about pregnancy and contraception, and family characteristics and dynamics of 100 teenage fathers were studied and compared with those of 100 nonfathers, age-matched peers in Memphis, Tennessee. Nearly all subjects were Black and were from families of low socioeconomic status. There were no differences between the two groups in age at first intercourse (mean 12.5 years) and frequency of intercourse in the last year. More control subjects than fathers perceived pregnancy as disruptive to their future plans for school, job, and marriage. The mothers of teen fathers were more likely to be teenaged mothers themselves. (77 percent versus 53 percent). In both groups, one third of their brothers and 44 percent of their sisters were teen parents. Both groups had poor knowledge about the risk of pregnancy and the effectiveness of contraceptives, and negative attitudes toward contraceptives. Both groups of subjects became sexually active at young ages, had poor knowledge of contraception, and often had unprotected intercourse. Although there were many similarities between the two groups, the teenage fathers seemed to come from environments in which teen pregnancy was common, accepted, and perceived as minimally disruptive to their lives now or in the future.

Scott-Jones, D., and Turner, S.L. (1988). Sex education, contraceptive and reproductive knowledge, and contraceptive use among Black adolescent females. *Journal of Adolescent Research, 3,* 171-187.

Demographic and social variables associated with beginning sexual activity were assessed in 114 Black and White males and females in early adolescence in a Southeastern city. Twenty-eight percent of the teens reported having had intercourse. There were not race or sex differences in sexual activity or age at first intercourse. Having a boyfriend or girlfriend, educational expectations, and age were significant predictors of sexual activity. For sexually active teens, race was the only significant predictor of regularity and effectiveness of contraception. For non-sexually active teens, boyfriend/girlfriend and age were significant predictors of noncoital sexual interactions.

Scott-Jones, D., and White, A.B. (in press). Correlates of sexual activity in early adolescence. *Journal of Early Adolescence.*

This study examined sources of sex education for Black adolescent females and assessed relationships among sex education, knowledge about contraception and reproduction, and contraceptive use, using data from the National Survey of Family Growth, Cycle III. The majority of teens reported having discussions with parents and having formal instruction about pregnancy, the menstrual cycle, and contraception. However, neither parental discussion nor formal instruction was related to reproductive knowledge, which was poor. A sample of older women had significantly greater reproductive knowledge than did the teens, although only one-fifth of the older women responded correctly. Formal instruction on contraception was positively related to contraceptive knowledge, which was positively associated with ever-use of contraception, use at first intercourse, current use, and effectiveness of current method. Age at first intercourse was a significant predictor of contraceptive use and effectiveness of current method.

Smith, E.A., and Udry, J.R. (1985). Coital and non-coital sexual behaviors of White and Black adolescents. *American Journal of Public Health, 75,* 1200-1203.

As part of a longitudinal study of young adolescents, data were collected in 1980 on the noncoital and coital sexual experiences of male and female adolescents who ranged in age from 12 to 15 at the time of the initial contact, and followed up two years later. Both Guttman scale analysis and a longitudinal analysis indicate different sexual patterns between White and Black teens: Whites are more likely than Blacks to engage in a predictable series of noncoital behaviors for a period of time before the first intercourse experience. These differences in sexual patterns were interpreted as offering a partial explanation for the different pregnancy rates between Black and White adolescents.

Sonenstein, F.L. (1987). Risking paternity: Sex and contraception among adolescent males. In M.E. Lamb and S. Elster (Eds.), *Adolescent fatherhood*. Hillsdale, N.J.: Lawrence Erlbaum.

This chapter summarizes the current state of knowledge about the incidence of adolescent fatherhood and the conditions leading to it. Research findings about sexual activity and contraceptive utilization are reviewed to identify factors associated with the early onset of sexual activity and the nonuse of contraceptives. In addition, potential intervention approaches designed to reduce adolescent pregnancy by involving male partners are discussed.

Westney, O.E., Jenkins, R.R., Butts, J.D., and Williams, I. (1984). Sexual development and behavior in Black adolescents. *Adolescence, 19,* 557-568.

As part of a longitudinal study of the sociosexual development of Black preadolescents, sexual maturation and sociosexual behavior were assessed in a sample of 101 nine to eleven-year-old middle and low income Black boys and girls in the Eastern U.S. Sexual maturation was assessed by Tanner's criteria, and heterosexual behaviors were classified on a five-point heterosexual physical activity (HPA) scale. The data corroborate other studies in demonstrating that girls were more advanced than boys in sexual maturation. Considerable variation in stages of maturation for chronological age existed in both boys and girls, but was more pronounced in girls. In girls, there was no significant association between HPA and degree of biological maturation. However, genital development in boys was significantly related to their sexual behavior. Income level was not associated with HPA score.

Williams-McCoy, J.E., and Tyler, F.B. (1985). Selected psychosocial characteristics of Black unwed adolescent fathers. *Journal of Adolescent Health Care, 6,* 12-16.

Adolescent fathers and nonfathers were compared as to their belief in a sense of personal control and responsibility for their lives (locus of control); ability to optimistically trust others (interpersonal trust); taking an active orientation toward life's demands and problems (coping style); and family/generational patterns of unwed parenthood. Participants were 24 unwed adolescent fathers and 27 unwed adolescent nonfathers, aged 15-19 years. Results suggest that adolescent fathers are usually older, more likely to have been born out-of-wedlock, and less trusting than nonfathers.

Zelnik, M., and Kantner, J.F. (1980). Sexual activity, contraceptive use and pregnancy among metropolitan teenagers: 1971-79. *Family Planning Perspectives, 12,* 231-238.

Surveys of national representative samples of females aged 15-19 and males aged 17-21 in 1979 indicate that somewhat higher proportions of Black adolescents have experienced sexual intercourse than have Whites. Among Black males, the rates were: age 17, 60.3 percent; 18, 78.8 percent; 19, 79.9 percent. Among Black females, the rates were: 15, 64.2 percent; 16, 41.0 percent; 17, 73.3 percent; 18, 76.3 percent; 19, 88.5 percent. Within age groups, the race difference was greater for females than for males. Thirty percent of Black adolescent females aged 15-19 had a pregnancy before marriage, while the rate among White adolescent females was 13.5 percent. Black females reported somewhat lower rates of contraceptive use than did White females. Other analyses are reported concerning the outcomes of pregnancy, pregnancy intentions, and specific contraceptive methods used.

Zelnik, M., Kantner, J.F., and Ford, K. (1981). *Sex and pregnancy in adolescence.* Beverly Hills, Calif.: Sage.

This research monograph analyzes 1971 and 1976 national surveys of adolescent females. It considers current age, SES, family stability, religion, religiosity, and age at menarche or first intercourse as predictors of: (1) sexual activity, (2) contraception, and (3) pregnancy. Comparisons of Blacks and Whites on these three outcome variables, adjusting for differences between these groups on demographic and other variables are presented.

Zelnik, M., and Shah, F.K. (1983). First intercourse among young Americans. *Family Planning Perspectives, 15,* 54-70.

Further analyses of the 1979 national survey by Zelnik and Kantner indicated that contraception is less often used in first intercourse by Black adolescent males and females than by Whites, but that Black adolescents used a medical method more often. A variety of other analyses, including many conducted separately within Blacks and Whites are reported.

Other References

Bauman, K., and Udry, R. (1972). Powerlessness and regularity of contraception in an urban Negro male sample: A research note. *Journal of Marriage and the Family, 34*(1), 112-114.

Bauman, K.E., and Udry, J.R. (1981). Subjective expected utility and adolescent sexual behavior. *Adolescence, 16,* 527-535.

Billy, J.O.G., and Udry, J.R. (1985). The influence of male and female best friends on adolescent sexual behavior. *Adolescence, 20,* 21-32.

Billy, J.O.G., and Udry, J.R. (1985). Patterns of adolescent friendship and effects on sexual behavior. *Social Psychology Quarterly, 48*(1), 27-41.

Brown, S.V. (1985). Premarital sexual permissiveness among Black adolescent females. *Social Psychology Quarterly, 48*(4), 180-192.

Butts, J.D. (1981). Adolescent sexuality and teenage pregnancy from a Black perspective. In T. Ooms (Ed.), *Teenage pregnancy in a family context* (pp.23-24). Philadelphia: Temple University.

Centers for Disease Control. (1986). Immunodeficiency syndrome (AIDS) among Blacks and Hispanics-United States. *MMWR, 35,* 655-666.

Chilman, C.S. (Ed.). (1980). *Adolescent sexuality in a changing society: Social and psychological perspectives.* (NIH Publication No. 80-1426.) Bethesda, Md.: National Institute of Child Health and Human Development.

Cohen, D.D., and Rose, R.K. (1984). Male adolescent birth control behavior: The importance of developmental factors and sex differences. *Journal of Youth and Adolescence, 13,* 239-252.

Delameter, J., and MacCorquodale, P. (1978). Premarital contraceptive use: A test of two models. *Journal of Marriage and the Family, 40,* 235-248.

DiClemente, R.J., Zorn, J., and Temoshok, L. (1986). Adolescents and AIDS: A survey of knowledge, beliefs and attitudes about AIDS in San Francisco. *American Journal of Public Health, 76,* 1443-1445.

DiClemente, R.J., Zorn, J., and Temshok, L. (1987). The association of gender, ethnicity, and length of residence in the Bay Area to adolescents' knowledge and attitudes about the acquired immune syndrome. *Journal of Applied Social Psychology, 17,* 193-215.

Dixon, R.D. (1980). The absence of birth order correlations among unwed and married Black first-contraceptors. *Journal of Sex Research, 16,* 238-244.

Eberhardt, C.A., and Schill, T. (1984). Differences in sexual attitudes and likeliness of sexual behaviors of Black lower-socioeconomic father-present vs. father-absent female adolescents. *Adolescence, 19,* 99-105.

Freeman, A.W., Rickels, K., Huggins, G.R., Mudd, E.H., Garcia, C., and Dickens, H.O. (1980). Adolescent contraceptive use: Comparisons of male and female attitudes and information. *American Journal of Public Health, 70,* 790-797.

Fox, G.L. (1977). Sex-role attitudes as predictors of contraceptive use among unmarried university students. *Sex Roles, 3,* 265-283.

Fox, G.L. (1986). Adolescent sex roles and sexuality. In G.R. Leigh and G.W. Peterson (Eds.) *Adolescents in Family Context* (pp. 179-204). Cincinnati: South-Western.

Graves, W., and Bradshaw, B.R. (1977). Early reconception and contraceptive use among Black teenage girls after an illegitimate birth. *American Journal of Public Health, 65*(7), 738-740.

Hammond, B., and Ladner, J. (1969). Socialization into sexual behavior in a Negro slum ghetto. In C.B. Broderick and J. Barnard (Eds.), *The individual, sex, and society* (pp. 41-51). Baltimore: Johns Hopkins.

Hendricks, L.E., and Fullilove, R.E. (1983). Locus of control and use of contraception among unmarried Black adolescent fathers and their controls: A preliminary report. *Journal of Youth and Adolescence, 12,* 225-233.

Ireson, C.J. (1984). Adolescent pregnancy and sex roles. *Sex Roles, 11,* 189-201.

James, W.R., Bernell, J., Walker, P., and Walker, E. (1977). Some problems of sexual growth in adolescent underprivileged unwed Black girls. *Journal of the National Medical Association, 69*(9), 631-33.

Koenig, M., and Zelnik, M. (1982). The risk of premarital first pregnancy among metropolitan-area teenagers: 1976 and 1979. *Family Planning Perspectives, 14,* 239-247.

MacAnarney, E., and Schreider, C. (1984). *Identifying social and psychological antecedents of adolescent pregnancy: The contribution of research to concepts of prevention.* New York: William T. Grant Foundation.

Moore, D.S., and Erickson, P.I. (1985). Age, gender, and ethnic differences in sexual and contraceptive knowledge, attitudes, and behaviors. *Family and Community Health* (November), 38-51.

Moore, K.A., and Burt, M.R. (1982). *Private crisis, public cost: Policy perspectives on teenage childbearing.* Washington: Urban Institute.

Nakashima, I., and Bonnie, B. (1984). Fathers of infants born to adolescent mothers: A study of paternal characteristics. *American Journal of the Developing Child, 138,* 452-454.

Namerow, P.E., and Jones, J.E. (1982). Ethnic variation in adolescent use of a contraceptive service. *Journal of Adolescent Health Care, 3,* 165-172.

Nathanson, C.A. (1985). The influence of client-provider relationships on teenage women's subsequent use of contraception. *American Journal of Public Health, 75,* 33-38.

O'Reilly, K.R., and Aral, S.O. (1985). Adolescence and sexual behavior: Trends and implications for STD. *Journal of Adolescent Care, 6,* 262-272.

Pleck, J.H., Sonenstein, F., and Swain, S.O. (1988). Adolescent males' sexual behavior and contraceptive use; Implications for male responsibility. *Journal of Adolescent Research, 3,* 275-284.

Redmond, M.A. (1985). Attitudes of adolescent males toward adolescent pregnancy and fatherhood. *Family Relations, 34,* 337-342.

Reiss, I.L., Banwart, A., and Foreman, H. (1975). Premarital contraceptive usage: A study and some theoretical explorations. *Journal of Marriage and the Family, 37,* 619-629.

Rivara, F.P., Sweeney, P.J., and Henderson, B.F. (1987). Risk of fatherhood among Black teenage males. *American Journal of Public Health, 77,* 203-205.

Russell-Briefel, R., Ezzati, T., and Perlman, J. (1985). Prevalence and trends in oral contraceptive use in premenopausal females ages 12-54 years, United States, 1971-80. *American Journal of Public Health, 75,* 1173-1176.

Thompson, L., and Spanier, G.B. (1978). Influence of parents, peers, and partners on the contraceptive use of college men and women. *Journal of Marriage and the Family, 40,* 481-492.

Ventura, S.J. (1984). Trends in teenage childbearing: United States, 1972-81. *Vital and Health Statistics, 21,* (September), i-iii, 1-22.

Zelnik, M., and Kantner, M. (1977). Sexual and contraceptive experiences of young unmarried women in the U.S.: 1971 and 1976. *Family Planning Perspectives, 9,* 55-71.

Zelnik, M., Koenig, M.A., and Kim, Y.J. (1984). Sources of prescription contraceptives and subsequent pregnancy among young women. *Family Planning Perspectives, 16,* 6-13.

Teen Parenting

JOYCE E. EVERETT
SMITH COLLEGE

Summary

Current statistics on the number of live births to women during adolescence has dramatically demonstrated the seriousness of teen pregnancy. Childbearing during this phase of the life course is correlated with special long- and short-term problems for the mother and child. Among these are the physical complications during the pregnancy and following the birth of the infant, as well as the psychological, social and economic consequences of teen parenthood. While investigations of the antecedents of a teen pregnancy are emerging, the study of the consequences of an adolescent pregnancy has lead many to conclude that ". . . the adolescent mother finds her life chances to be truncated" (Brooks-Gunn and Furstenberg, 1986).

Recently, physicians, psychologists and others have developed increasing concern about the differences in development among children born to adolescent and nonadolescent parents. Generally, the dissimilarities in the development of the children born to adolescent and nonadolescent mothers are presumably explained by differences in the childrearing behaviors and practices of the child's parents. Among Black adolescents, teen parenting practices are particularly important because of (1) the disproportionately high rate of out-of-wedlock births, (2) the cognitive and behavioral difficulties reported among the school-aged children of this population, and (3) the implications for social policies aimed toward alleviating the economic, educational, and psychological consequences of teen pregnancy and parenting.

Conceptually, the parenting behaviors and practices among adolescent and adult parents result from differences in stress and coping, social support, cognitive development, attitudes toward childrearing, knowledge of child development, and actual behaviors toward the child. Much of this research has been conducted with adolescent primiparas. Throughout the literature, two underlying themes emerge: (1) that only slight differences in the infant parenting behaviors of teenage and older mothers have been observed; and, (2) that teen fathers are neither willing nor prepared to assume a responsible parenting role and are in fact marginal participants in the rearing of their children. Several studies show that teen mothers vocalize less to their children than other mothers; have less realistic expectations about their children's developmental progress; have less knowledge about child development than their older counterparts; and, were initially unhappy about their pregnancy. Few studies examine the effects of teenage motherhood on a subsequent birth.

Methodological shortcomings are common in this research area. Among the problems evidenced are the use of comparable samples of older mothers; sample attrition especially in studies of teen mothers and their infants over time; and rater bias. Comparisons across studies are problematic due to several inconsistencies in the methodologies used, including: (1) variations in the manner in which researchers operationalize variables such as the age of the mother (e.g., whether age of mother at first birth or age of mother at birth of the index child), (2) differences in the categorizations of intervening variables such as family background, birth order, or family size, (4) differences in the utilization of control variables such as socioeconomic status, (5) differences in the use of standard measures as opposed to self reports or parent and teacher reports of behavior, and (6) the inclusion of separate analyses by race and sex.

The current rate of teen pregnancy clearly warrants a systematic study of teen parenting practices and the consequences for young children. Longitudinal and cross-sectional studies might suggest how changes in the parent's life (e.g., marriage, divorce, completion of school, support from grandparents and others) influence parenting practices and the child. Larger sample sizes, the use of control variables and separate analyses of racial and sex groupings would further understanding of the parenting issues for this population.

Annotated References

Boxhill, N. (1987). How would you feel. . . ?: Clinical interviews with black adolescent mothers. *Child and Youth Services, 9*(1), 41-51.

The experiences of twelve poor, black adolescent mothers between the ages of 16 and 19 as reported during clinical interviews over an eight month period are described in this article. Each of the 12 black mothers was interviewed at least seven times for approximately 45 minutes. Descriptions of their growing years, decision-making processes, experiences of parenting as well as feelings and beliefs about their futures were solicited during these interviews. Four themes emerged from this phenomenological investigation, including: (1) the perceived failures of their own parents; (2) a lack of satisfactory intimate relations with peers and others; (3) the experience of being simultaneously too young and too old; and, (4) the challenge of becoming a good mother. The author draws implications from these findings for clinicians working with this population, service providers, program planning and implementation of adolescent pregnancy programs.

Brooks-Gunn, J., and Furstenberg, F.F. (1986). The children of adolescent mothers: Physical, academic, and psychological outcome. *Developmental Psychology, 6,* 225-251.

In this review of the literature, a series of issues regarding the consequences of teenage parenthood for children are examined including: (1) the areas of a child's development that are affected; (2) the ages at which negative effects appear; (3) differences in negative consequences for boys and girls; and (4) the antecedents of deleterious child outcomes. The review explores individual differences in the expression of parenting by different-aged mothers by focusing on two questions: how do parenting patterns originate and how do parental practices affect the young child's social, physical, and cognitive development. Though a paucity of empirical data exists on these topics, the findings suggest that teenage mothers vocalize less to their children than do older parents; that teenage mothers appear to have less realistic expectations than older mothers with regard to their children's developmental progress; that teenage mothers are not more depressed than older mothers; that high support and personal control reduced the impact of negative life events significantly; that the effects of teenage childbearing, when found, are mediated by factors such as education, single-parent households and family size; and, finally, that intellectual differences in children of teenage and older childbearers become more pronounced as children develop. The investigators conclude that these issues require systematic study with more representative samples of teenage mothers.

Brown, S. (1983). The commitment and concerns of Black adolescent parents. *Social Work Research and Abstracts, 19*(4), 27-34.

This article reports on a study of Black adolescent fathers and mothers which assessed the quality of their commitment and concerns as a couple. Using the couple as the primary unit of analysis, Brown assesses the attitudes of young Black expectant parents to determine how they diverge from those generally assumed in the literature. The data for this study were collected from a nonprobability sample of 36 Black expectant adolescent couples at the Maternal and Child Health Clinic in Baltimore. Personal interviews were conducted with each partner to elicit information about each partner's perception of the couple's relationship; attitudes and behaviors concerning premarital sexual intercourse and their forthcoming parenting responsibilities. The analysis showed that sexual values vary among lower-class Black youth; that the level of commitment of the couples could be determined by knowing how each partner felt about the other prior to the pregnancy and whether their feelings were mutual; and, that the two most frequently cited concerns of the expectant parents were their ability to assume future financial responsibilities and not being able to go out and have fun after the child's birth. Brown provides an adequate critique of the limitations of this study and discusses the implications of the findings for future research and service delivery.

Card, J.J. (1981). Long-term consequences for children of teenage parents. *Demography, 18*(2), 137-156.

In this publication, Card investigates the long-term outcomes for children born when their mother and/or father was an adolescent. The data base for the analysis, Project TALENT, was a longitudinal national survey of 375,000 individuals who were in grades 9-12 in 1960. In this analysis, TALENT participants born when their mother and/or father was a teenager were compared with their classmates born when both parents were older. Controlling for background factors, Card's findings indicate that children of teenage parents, in comparison to their classmates showed: (a) a greater probability of living in a nonintact home in high school: (b) lower academic aptitude as a teenager; and (c) a slightly increased probability of repeating the parent's pattern of early marriage, early parenthood and greater fertility. Card concludes by emphasizing the importance of a stable, continuous family environment for the intellectual growth of children.

Elster, A., McAnarney, E., and Lamb, M. (1983). Parental behavior of adolescent mothers. *Pediatrics, 71*(4), 494-503.

This paper reviews the literature on the parental behavior of adolescent parents. More specifically, the studies reviewed focus on the various modes by which parents interact with their infants, the association between stress, coping, social support, cognitive development, attitudes toward childrearing, knowledge of child development, and characteristics of the infant, as factors, influence the responsivity of adolescent parenting. Particular attention is given to studies regarding the association between child abuse and suboptimal cognitive development and adolescent parenthood.

Field, T., Widmayer, S., Stringer, S., and Ignatoff, E. (1980). Teenage, lower-class, Black mothers and their preterm infants: An intervention and developmental follow-up. *Child Development, 51,* 426-436.

This article presents the analysis from a study designed to follow the development of preterm and full-term infants born to teenage versus adult mothers belonging to a lower socioeconomic group and to assess the effects of an intervention provided to a subsample of the preterm infants born to teenage mothers. The sample consisted of 150 randomly selected experimental and control infants and their lower-class, Black mothers. The experimental group received home-based parent training. Assessments were made at four-month intervals to compare the development of term and preterm infants born to adult and teenage mothers to evaluate the effects of the intervention. Infants of teenage mothers appeared to be at greater risk by virtue of their small-for-date size at birth and their mother's less realistic developmental expectations, less desirable child-rearing attitudes, and less optimal evaluation of their temperaments.

Fu, V., Hinkle, D., Shoffner, S., Carter, S., Clark, A., Culley, P., Disney, G., Ercanli, G., Glover, E., Kenney, M., Lewis, H., Moak, S., Stalling, S., and Wakefield, T. (1984). Maternal dependency and childrearing attitudes among mothers of adolescent females. *Adolescence, 19*(76), 795-804.

This study examined the differences in childrearing attitudes among 964 Black and White mothers of adolescent females from different ethnic and social class backgrounds. Subjects were recruited through school systems in eight southern states. The results indicate significant differences between Black and White mothers on four measures of childrearing attitudes: fostering dependency, excluding outside influences, encouraging independence, and loyalty to parents. Black mothers had higher mean scores than the White mothers on all four measures. The findings also suggest that childrearing attitudes do not differ significantly between mothers of younger and older adolescent girls.

Furstenberg, F.F. (1980). Burdens and benefits: The impact of early childbearing on the family. *Journal of Social Issues, 36*(1), 64-87.

The purpose of this analysis was to explore the effects of teenage pregnancy and childbearing on families-of-origin and to examine the amount and type of support provided by the family to the pregnant teenager. Data were obtained from two primary sources: a secondary analysis of data from a longitudinal study conducted in Baltimore from 1967 to 1972 with a total of 320 women (mostly Black) and data collected during a pilot study with 15 families (nine Black, three White, and three Hispanic) in Philadelphia. Data from the longitudinal study were used to provide a demographic overview of the residential patterns of adolescent mothers following the birth of the first child, while information from the pilot study was used to offer a more microscopic view of the family support process. Based on the data, the findings indicate the mothers were more likely to receive substantial amounts of financial assistance and child care when they remained with relatives. The most common residential pattern among pregnant mothers was unbroken residence with the family of origin. While age was not strongly related to the young mother's continuing residence with her parents, educational status, the bond between parent and daughter, and the adolescent mother's level of dependency were better predictors of residential patterns. Adolescents who remained with their parents were more likely to advance educationally and economically as compared with their peers who left home. The microscopic view gleaned from interviews with teen mothers and family members suggest tremendous variations in the division of labor among families, an elevation of the status of the young mother in the family, and a repositioning of the status of other family members.

Furstenberg, F.F., and Talvitic, K. (1980). Children's names and paternal claims. *Journal of Family Issues, 1*(1), 31-57.

In this paper, Furstenberg and Talvitic explore the paternal involvement of fathers who do not reside with their offspring during the first five years of the child's life. These data are contrasted with data on males who were married to the mother of their child during the same time period. The respondents in this study were the male partners of 323 unmarried teenage mothers who participated in a longitudinal study conducted in Baltimore over a five-year period. The analysis tends to focus on the manner in which naming patterns structure and reinforce familial bonds. The results show a consistent association between naming patterns and paternal involvement in the families of never-married fathers. When children bore their father's name (nearly two-thirds of the sons and almost half the daughters did), they were much more likely to have regular contact with their fathers and to receive economic assistance from them. Despite this overall finding the authors caution against making the assertion that a direct causal link exists between naming patterns and child development. Instead the authors conclude that naming patterns expressed potential commitment to paternity.

McAnarney, E., Lawrence, R., Ricciuti, H., Polley, J., and Szilagyi, M. (1986). Interactions of adolescent mothers and their one-year old children. *Pediatrics, 78*(4), 585-590.

The purpose of this study was to examine the relationship between adolescent maternal age and the nature of the behavioral interaction between mothers and their children. Twenty minute videotaped behavioral observations of the parent-child interactions of 30 medically and psychologically normal adolescent mothers and their 9- and 12-month-old children were the basis for this study. The sample consisted of

Black, White, and Puerto Rican adolescent mothers between the ages of 15 and 20 years. Rating scales measuring the quality of mother-child attachment, the quality of interactive behavior and child behavior were used by trained coders to score structured and unstructured sequences of the videotaped behaviors. Findings based on Pearson correlation show that younger adolescent mothers tended to be less accepting, less cooperative, less accessible, less sensitive, and engaged in negative verbal communication with their children. A modest but significant relationship was found between (1) young adolescent maternal age and quality of verbal communication, and (2) maternal age and children's behavior. Children of younger adolescent mothers were less likely to initiate social contact with their mother than were the children of older adolescent mothers. The authors speculate that the cognitive and behavioral problems of the school-aged children of adolescents may originate in these maternal-child interactive behaviors approximately one year after birth and recommend early intervention as a preventive measure.

Osofsky, H., and Osofsky, J. (1970). Adolescents as mothers. *American Journal of Orthopsychiatry, 40*(5), 825-834.

Results from an evaluation of an interdisciplinary program for pregnant adolescents and their infants are reported in this article. The program, Young Mothers Education Development, uniquely housed in a school building provided a wide range of services including medical care, education, a nursery facility, social and psychological services, and a cooperative kitchen and cafeteria. Data were on the obstetrical, nutritional, social, and educational status of the girls participating in the program during and following delivery. Approximately 62 percent of the participants in the program were nonwhite. Follow-up visits on well and sick babies were conducted at monthly intervals for the first six-months and at three month intervals thereafter. Observational data of mother-infant interaction were videotaped at all pediatric visits before and during examination. Infant behavior was rated on a 5-point scale for the amount of activity. Rating of the mother's behavior on a 5-point scale assessed the amount of verbal interaction and physical interaction with the child as well as warmth. Findings indicate that the mothers rate high on measures of warmth and physical interaction and low on measures of verbal interaction.

Parke, R., Power, T., and Fisher, T. (1980). The adolescent father's impact on the mother and child. *Journal of Social Issues, 36*(1), 88-106.

Empirical studies conducted between 1968 and 1980 regarding the nature of the father-infant relationship, the impact of the father on the infant's social and cognitive development and the effect of the father on the mother and on her relationship with the infant are examined in this article. The review of these studies indicate that teenagers (mothers and fathers) are limited in their knowledge of infant development. Though studies of adolescent father-infant play are sparse, such studies with samples of older fathers suggest differences in the play patterns of fathers and mothers. Furthermore, infants respond differently to maternal and paternal play behavior. Fathers' physical play best predicted boys' cognitive development, while the quality of the father's verbal interaction was a better predictor for female cognitive status. These authors conclude with a discussion of the nature of cultural support systems that may help foster greater involvement among adolescent fathers with their children.

Presser, H. (1980). Sally's corner: Coping with unmarried motherhood. *Journal of Social Issues, 36*(1), 107-129.

In this article Presser focuses on the coping strategies of a sample of unmarried mothers beginning with the first child. She examines the support systems these mothers rely on and changes in these systems over time. The data presented in this analysis are based on a subsample of 69 unmarried women drawn from a larger sample of 408 women who were randomly selected from three boroughs in New York City (i.e., Brooklyn, the Bronx, and Queens). Each woman was interviewed three times, in-person and by telephone between 1973 and 1976. More than three-fourths of the 69 women were Black and Protestant. Presser notes an increase in nonfamilial (e.g., returning to school or work) and familial role responsibilities following the birth of the child among unmarried mothers. While the families-of-origin were found to provide assistance to these women, relatively few unmarried fathers provided assistance in a major way with the day-to-day demands of childrearing. Of those fathers who did provide assistance, the data showed that their assistance tapered off with time. Fathers who wanted to marry the child's mothers were more likely to contribute to the child's support than were other fathers. Unmarried mothers who remained with their parents following the birth of their first child were more likely to return to school. Presser concludes by raising several policy issues regarding familial support and preventive measures.

Sawin, D.B., and Parke, R.D. (1976). Adolescent fathers: Some implications from recent research on paternal roles. *Educational Horizons, 55,* 36-43.

This article examines the available research on paternal roles and father-infant interaction and discusses the implications of this work for adolescent fathers and professionals in education and health-care delivery. The review of empirical studies focused on several key questions including: (1) Are fathers less active in care-giving with their newborn infants than mothers? (2) Does the father's involvement affect the mother's behavior with their infants? and, (3) Are fathers less competent care-givers than mothers? The findings indicate the fathers are equally as active as mothers in their social activities with their infants, and that the father's active participation in interactions within the triad (e.g., mother-infant-father) serve to enhance the mother's interest in the infant. The investigators conclude that childbirth among adolescents should not be encouraged; however, where conception has occurred, opportunities for adolescent fathers to fulfill their parental roles should be encouraged.

Stevens, J., and Duffield, B. (1986). Age and parenting skill among Black women in poverty. *Early Childhood Research Quarterly, 1,* 221-235.

A total of 158 low-income Black mothers and their infants were recruited to take part in a study of the relationship between mother's age and measures of various dimensions of maternal behavior. Observational techniques and interviews were used as the primary methods for data collection. The results of the study indicate that mother's age is related to parenting behavior. Younger mothers were observed to show less responsive and more punitive interactive behavior and were less able to support the intellectual development of their infants than older mothers.

Sullivan, M.L. (1984). *Teen fathers in the inner city.* New York: Vera Institute of Justice.

The data presented in this report on fathering describe youth from one of three neighborhoods in New York City. The study, an ethnographic observational study, was designed to describe and explore some of the ways in which the rights and duties of teen fatherhood are established and maintained. Eleven youth, mostly Black adolescent males, were interviewed to obtain a detailed life-history concerning their family backgrounds, social and sexual development, and patterns of fathering. Though the sample size is small, the findings suggest a diversity of arrangements for child care and financial support. Child care was provided by both parents, grandparents and other relatives. Some fathers made regular contributions of income from their criminal activity, while others found jobs and provided support for as long as employment remained steady. Several mothers and fathers were completing their education and taking advantage of community health and nutritional programs. The results of the study were interpreted as an indication that a great deal of child support by unmarried teen fathers is concealed from public scrutiny and further study is necessary.

Thompson, M. (1986). The influence of supportive relations on the psychological well-being of teenage mothers. *Social Forces, 64*(4), 1006-1024.

This article examines the impact of family and peer resources on adjustment of teenage mothers by investigating the relationship between different sources of social support and perceptions of maternal stress and psychological distress. Interviews were conducted with a sample of 296 mothers who delivered a first child between September, 1978 and August, 1979. The sample was drawn from the delivery records of a large urban general hospital. The majority of the sampled mothers were Black, (64 percent Black, 30 percent White, and 6 percent Hispanic) and single, with a median age of 17 at the birth of the child. Information was elicited on the mothering experience, availability of help from others, and the infant's health through structured interviews conducted in the mothers' homes. Analysis of these data suggest an important racial difference in the coping responses of teenage mothers, with White females being more likely to report stress with mothering than Black females. Self-reports of stress and difficulties in fulfilling mothering duties were higher for those women who received help from friends or from relatives than for those who did not. Moreover, self-reports of psychological distress were lower for young mothers who received support from a husband, male companion, or the infant's father than for those who did not. The investigator concludes that the study confirms a multidimensional explanation of social supports and racial differences in coping responses of teenage mothers. Social supports were not uniformly positive: some significant others had positive effects on well-being while others showed negative effects on well-being.

Williams, R. (1974). Childrearing practices of young mothers. *Journal of Orthopsychiatry, 44*(1), 70-75.

This article assesses the reasons for the lack of research on young single-parents and multiple care-givers and offers suggestions for the direction of future studies. A brief discussion of the preliminary data comparing infant attachment behaviors toward single mothers is also presented.

Zuckerman, B., Winsmore, G., and Alpert, J. (1979). A study of attitudes and support systems of inner-city adolescent mothers. *Journal of Pediatrics, 95*(1), 122-125.

This article focuses on the attitudes and support systems available to adolescent mothers during the early adjustment of the mother to her infant. The sample consisted of a total of 55 mother-infant pairs selected on the second or third postpartum day. Twenty-three of these women were under the age of 18; eight were older than 21; and 24 were women over the age 21 who gave birth to more than one child at the time of delivery. Each mother was interviewed twice; once two weeks after delivery and again three months following delivery. Most of the mothers were Black and their babies males. Few of the mothers were married (8 percent). Of those not married, most (95 percent) lived in an extended family. Adolescent mothers were more likely to seek medical advice from their mothers than older mothers. The majority of the sampled mothers stated that the father was helping with the baby when first interviewed. Compared to the other two groups, more adolescent mothers expressed insecurity about their role as a mother. Moreover, more adolescent mothers were concerned about whether the baby would recognize them as the mother if care-taking was shared with another person.

Other References

Teen Parenting

Battle, S.F. (1987). *The Black adolescent parent.* New York: Haunorth.

Bolton, F.G., Laner, R., and Kane, S. (1980). Child maltreatment risk among adolescent mothers: A study of reported cases. *American Journal of Orthopsychiatry, 50*(3), 489-504.

Jones, F., Green, V., and Krauss, D. (1980). Maternal responsiveness of primiparous mothers during the postpartum period: Age differences. *Pediatrics, 65*(3), 579-584.

Kinard, E.M., and Klerman, L. (1980). Teenage pregnancy and child abuse: Are they related? *American Journal of Orthopsychiatry, 50*(3), 481-488.

Lamb, M., and Elster, A. (1985). Adolescent mother-infant-father relationships. *Developmental Psychology, 21*(5), 768-773.

Levine, L., Coll, C.T., and Oh, W. (1985). Determinants of mother-infant interaction in adolescent mothers. *Pediatrics, 75*(1), 23-29.

Olson, S., Bates, J.E., and Bayles, K. (1984). Mother-infant interaction and the development of individual differences in children's cognitive competence. *Developmental Psychology, 20*(1), 166-179.

Ragozin, A.S., Basham, R.B., Crnic, K.A., Greenberg, M.T., and Robinson, N. (1982). Effects of maternal age on parenting role. *Developmental Psychology, 18*(4), 627-634.

Roosa, M., Fitzgerald, H., and Carson, N.A. (1982). Teenage and older mothers and their infants: A description comparison. *Adolescence, 17*(65), 1-17.

Stevens, J.H. (1984). Black grandmothers' and black adolescent mothers' knowledge about parenting. *Developmental Psychology, 20*(6), 1017-1025.

Stevens, J.H. (1984). Child development knowledge and parenting skills. *Family Relations, 33*(1), 237-244.

Wilson, M. (1986). Perceived parental activity of mothers, fathers, and grandmothers in three-generational black families. *Journal of Black Psychology, 12*(2), 43-59.

Wise, S., and Grossman, F. (1980). Adolescent mothers and their infants: Psychological factors in early attachment and interaction. *American Journal of Orthopsychiatry, 50*(3), 454-468.

Zeanah, C., Keener, M., Anders, T., and Vierira-Baker, C. (1987). Adolescent mothers' perceptions of their infants before and after birth. *American Journal of Orthopsychiatry, 57*(3), 351-359.

Teen Pregnancy

Black, C. and DeBlassie, R. (1985). Adolescent pregnancy: Contributing factors, consequences and plausible solutions. *Adolescence, 22.*

Brown, S. (1983). The commitment and concerns of black adolescent parents. *Social Work Research and Abstracts, 19*(4), 27-34.

Card, J.J., and Wise, L.L.(1978). Teenage mothers and teenage fathers. *Family Planning Perspectives, 10,* 199-205.

Colletta, N., and Lee, D. (1983). Impact of support for Black adolescent mothers. *Journal of Family Issues, 4*(1), 127-143.

Franklin, D.L. (1987). Black adolescent pregnancy: A literature review. *Child and Youth Services, 9*(1), 15-39.

Furstenberg, F. (1980). Burdens and benefits: The impact of early childbearing on the family. *Journal of Social Issues, 36*(1), 64-87.

Furstenberg, F.F., Brooks-Gunn, J., and Morgan, S.P. (1987). *Adolescent mothers in later life.* New York: Cambridge University.

Furstenberg, F., and Crawford, A. (1987). Family support: Helping teenage mothers to cope. *Family Planning Perspectives, 10*(6), 322-333.

Furstenberg, F.F., Lincoln, R., and Menen, J. (Eds.), (1981). *Teenage sexuality, pregnancy and childbearing.* Philadelphia: University of Pennsylvania.

Goodwin, N.J. (1986). Black adolescent pregnancy: Prevention and management (Special Issue). *Journal of Community Health, 11*(1).

Morgan, P, and Waite, L. (1987). Parenthoood and the attitudes of young adults. *American Sociological Review, 52,* 541-547.

Russell, C. (1980). Unscheduled parenthood: Transition to 'parent' for the teenager. *Journal of Social Issues, 36*(1), 45-63.

Scott-Jones, D., Roland, E.J., and White, A.B. (1989). In R. Jones, (Ed.), *Black Adolescents* (pp. 341-371). Berkeley: Cobb & Henry.

Teen Fathers

Barret, R.L., and Robinson, B.E. (1986). Adolescent fathers: Often forgotten parents. *Pediatric Nursing, 12*(4), 273-277.

Barret, R., and Robinson, B.E. (1982). Teenage fathers: Neglected too long. *Social Work, 27*(6), 484-488.

Barth, R.P., Claycomb, M., and Loomis, A. (1988). Services to adolescent fathers. *Health and Social Work, 13*(4), 277-287.

Hendricks, L., Howard, C., and Caesar, P. (1981). Help-seeking behavior among select populations of Black unmarried adolescent fathers. *American Journal of Public Health, 71*(7), 733-735.

Honig, A.S., and Wayne, G. (1982). Black fathering in three social class groups. *Ethnic Groups, 4,* 229-238.

Klinman, D., and Sander, J.H. (1985). *Reaching and serving the teenage father.* New York: Bank Street College of Education.

Nakashima, I., and Camp, B. (1984). Fathers of infants born to adolescent mothers. *AJDC, 136,* 452-454.

Redmond, M. (1985). Attitudes of adolescent males toward adolescent pregnancy and fatherhood. *Family Relations, 34,* 337-342.

Rivera, F., Sweeney, P., and Henderson, B. (1985). A study of low socioeconomic status, Black teenage fathers and their nonfather peers. *Pediatrics, 75,* 648-656.

Rivara, S., Sweeney, P., and Henderson, B. (1987). Risks of fatherhood among Black teenage males. *American Journal of Public Health, 77*(2), 203-205.

Robinson, B.E. (1980). Teenage pregnancy from the father's perspective. *American Journal of Orthopsychiatry, 58*(1), 46-51.

Vaz, R., Smolen, P., and Miller, C. (1983). Adolescent pregnancy: Involvement of the male partner. *Journal of Adolescent Health Care, 4*(4), 246-250.

Williams-McCoy, J., and Tyler, F. (1985). Selected psychosocial characteristics of black unwed adolescent fathers. *Journal of Adolescent Health Care, 6*(1), 12-16.

Child Support

Beller, A., and Graham, J. (1986). Child support awards: Differentials and trends by race and marital status. *Demography, 23*(2), 231-245.

Cutright, P. (1986). Child support and responsible male procreative behavior. *Sociological Focus, 19*(1), 27-43.

Danziger, S.K., and Nichols-Casebolt, A. (1988). Teen parents, and child support: eligibility, participation and payment. *Journal of Social Service Research, 11*(2/3), 1-19.

Everett, J. (1981). *The merits of child support payments as an income source for female-headed households.* (Working Paper No. 75.) Wellesley, Mass.: Wellesley College Center for Research on Women.

Everett, J. (1984). *The impact of child support enforcement actions on compliance behavior and the relationships among disrupted family members.* Unpublished doctoral dissertation, Brandeis University, The Florence Heller School of Social Welfare.

Everett, J. (1985). An examination of child support enforcement issues. In H. McAdoo and T.M.J. Parham (Eds.), *Services to Young Families* (pp. 75-112). Washington, D.C.: *American Public Welfare.*

Everett, J. (1987). *Final report of the Maryland Child Support Enforcement Research Project.* Baltimore, Md.: Department of Human Resources, Office of the Executive Director, Maryland Child Support Enforcement Administration.

Nichols-Casebolt, A. (1986). Economic impact of child support reform on the poverty status of custodial and noncustodial fathers. *Journal of Marriage and the Family, 48,* 875-880.

Nichols-Casebolt, A. (1988). Paternity adjudication: In the best interests of the out-of-wedlock child. *Child Welfare, 67*(3), 245-254.

Rivera-Casale, C., Klerman, L., and Manela, R. (1984). The relevance of child support enforcement to school-age parents. *Child Welfare, 63*(6), 521-531.

Wattenberg, E. (1984). *Project on paternity and adjudication and child support obligations of teenage parents.* Minneapolis: University of Minnesota, Center for Urban and Regional Affairs.

Wright, D., and Price, S. (1986). Court-ordered child support payment: The effect of the former-spouse relationship on compliance. *Journal of Marriage and the Family, 48,* 869-874.

Contributors' Notes

The Consortium for Research on Black Adolescence is composed of eight researchers:

Patricia Bell-Scott (Project Director), Associate Professor, Human Development and Family Relations, University of Connecticut. Her interests include family-adolescent relationships and female gender role development.

Joyce E. Everett, Assistant Professor, Smith College School of Social Work. Her interests include teen parenthood, child support, substitute care, and adoption.

Carol J. Carter, Coordinator of Research, Division of Student Affairs, Northeastern University. Her interests include the career and occupational education of girls, as well as professional and leadership development among women.

Patrick C. McKenry, Professor, Family Relations and Human Development, The Ohio State University, Columbus, Ohio. His interests include adolescent depression, drug abuse, pregnancy, and suicide, as well as divorce, stress, and coping.

Joseph H. Pleck, Henry Luce Professor of Families, Change and Society, Wheaton College. His interests include contraception, adolescent sexuality, teen parenthood, male roles, and work-family issues.

Saundra Murray Nettles, Principal Research Scientist, Center for the Social Organization of Schools, The Johns Hopkins University. Her interests include achievement behavior in disadvantaged youth, as well as applied research that identifies, describes, and evaluates community based methods for preventing adolescent crises.

Howard P. Ramseur, Clinical Psychologist, Medical Department, the Massachusetts Institute of Technology. His interests include psychological health, the development of racial identity, and psychosocial aspects of academic achievement.

Ronald L. Taylor (Project Co-Director), Associate Professor, Sociology, University of Connecticut. His interests include the impact of significant others on psychosocial development and role modeling behavior, as well as value and political orientations among youth.

Other contributors to this work include:

Velma McBride Murry, Assistant Professor, Human Development and Family Relations, University of Connecticut. Her interests include adolescent sexuality and parenthood, as well as stress and coping.

Georgie Winter, Research Assistant to CROBA and doctoral student in the School of Family Studies, University of Connecticut. Her interests include the development and maintenance of control beliefs, and the role of self-esteem and self-efficacy beliefs in the stress and coping process.